Lewis Dayton Burdick

Through Field and Wood

Lyric verses and sonnets

Lewis Dayton Burdick

Through Field and Wood
Lyric verses and sonnets

ISBN/EAN: 9783744758499

Printed in Europe, USA, Canada, Australia, Japan

Cover: Foto ©Thomas Meinert / pixelio.de

More available books at **www.hansebooks.com**

Through Field and Wood.

Lyric Verses and Sonnets.

BY

LEWIS DAYTON BURDICK.

PHILADELPHIA:

J. B. LIPPINCOTT COMPANY.

1888.

CONTENTS.

SONGS OF LOVE.

SONGS OF FLOWERS.

DEVOTIONAL.

SONNETS.

BALLADS, RONDEAUS, AND TRIOLETS.

THE COMING OF WINTER.

GRIM sentinels, majestic, silent stand the naked
 beeches;
 The balsams stagger with their burdens of new-
  fallen snow;
 The sombre clouds above reach down to sombre
  woods below,
Along the line of distant hills far as the vision
 reaches.

The south wind whispers through the lonesome
 tamarack its warnings;
 On lilac bough the nest hangs tenantless, and
  capped with snow,
 Which bluebirds built among the scented blos-
  soms long ago,
When they beneath my window sang and wooed on
 May-day mornings.

Beneath the shed's low eaves the homes are crumb-
    ling of the swallows;
  The barn-yard's sunny side the ruminating kine
    seek out,
  And all day long the lazy creatures hardly turn
    about;
The trodden snow-path daintily the vane-cock
    closely follows:

The fences on the broad white fields are pencil lines
    one fancies;
  Upon the pansy-beds are spread soft coverlets of
    snow;
  The ice creeps in the coves where sluggishly the
    waters flow,
And stealthily into the middle of the stream ad-
    vances.

The steel-shod sled again the boys bring from the
    kitchen garret;
  Once more are oiled and strapped and polished
    up the rusting skates;
  With muffled ears they brave the night to seek
    the joy that waits,
And were the cold ten times as great, unflinching
    they would bear it.

Acquaintances meet on the street, and pass with
    hurried paces;
  And there they meet, from fireless homes and
    palaces of gold;
  The warmth of wool and wealth of seal shield
    one from pinching cold,—
Her sisters follow with want written on their pallid
    faces.

Now silence reigns in haunts once musical with
    many voices;
  The sun at noon but half way to the zenith
    climbs; ah, me,
What restfulness there is in ˙Nature's inactivity!
The weary brain and weary limb her sympathy
    rejoices.

And still, the coming of the winter always brings a
    sadness
  Akin to that of parting with a friend we long
    have known;
  Or that of leaving some familiar place dear to us
    grown,
For which a longing afterwards sometimes comes in
    our gladness.

Springtime's attractive grace, the richness of the
    riper season,
  And all the tragic glory of the autumn days yet
    cling
  To memory, and yet for them our hearts are
    hungering;
But how considerate and kind is Nature, and what
    reason,

If we but think of it, once more she gives us to be
    grateful;
  For she embalms her dead with older than
    Egyptian rite,
  As tenderly and lovingly she covers from the
    sight
Of men, with her broad mantle of soft ermine, all
    things hateful.

And with that trusting faith true children of
    Osiris waited
  For their lost friends, in other forms, to come to
    them again,
  We know the sweet influences of summer's
    warmth and rain
Will bring again the leaves and flowers reformed
    and sublimated.

Both in her toil and rest, what lessons Nature to us
    teaches!
  Oh, stony, grinding greed! oh, blind, insatiate
    avarice!
  Behold, how free the fragrance borne on every
    zephyr is!
Or how the tree casts off the crown of splendor that
    it reaches,

And in its garb of faded sackcloth winter's storming
    faces,
  As if submitting meekly to be scourged, in peni-
    tence,
  For too unseemly pride, arrayed in its magnifi-
    cence;
And yet, withal, the coming of the winter brings its
    graces.

Although into some homes want creeps with the
    inclement weather,
  From hearths and hearts grown cold some fire
    Love from the embers rakes,
  Which warmth and blessing has for him who
    gives and him who takes,
And once more human needs bring human hearts
    more close together.

As simplest plant that blooms and dies, its life one
    summer ending,
  And that whose gorgeous crown comes only with
    a century,
  Fulfil God's purposes, we know, though how we
    may not see,
That for our good the winter's frown and summer's
    smile are blending.

I hear the crazy wind, and tremble at its visitation,
  Yet germs of pestilence it sweeps away from me,
    maybe;
  The pollen of the clover revels in, for greed, the
    bee,
But life and death of crimson fields hang on his
    ministration.

Oh, white-winged hosts down from the frosted
    storm-clouds wildly flying,
  Are ye the guardian ghosts of rays of all the
    daisies past,
  Come hovering o'er to shield the sod from the
    northwester's blast?
Beneath the crystal mountains summer's bloom is
    fallow lying.

It is not death the winter brings; beyond I see the
    meadows
  Greening; afar I catch the odor of the violet;
  There is no death; our loved and lost are only
    sleeping yet,
And we shall grasp them by the hand beyond the
    darksome shadows.

A DAY.

THE day is breaking in the east:
    What will it bring?
More depth of woe, some added bitterness,
    One friendship ceased,
A few sad anxious hours whose lingering
Subdues the strength and makes the faith grow less,—
    What will it bring?

The day is breaking in the east:
    What will it bring?
Some sweeter harmony of reed or lyre
    For soul to feast
Upon? To satisfy heart's hungering,
Some dear fulfilment of its fond desire,—
    What will it bring?

The day is breaking in the east:
　　What will it bring?
Joy to some captive from his galling chain
　　At length released,
The throning in some heart of love as king,
Awaking to his rapture and his pain,—
　　What will it bring?

The day is dying in the west:
　　What has it brought?
More wealth of hope, a touch of tenderness,
　　One wrong confessed,
Some aspiration lifting higher, one thought
Some fragment of humanity will bless,—
　　What has it brought?

The day is dying in the west:
　　What has it brought?
Some friend estranged to sup and taste our wine,
　　A welcome guest?
Some strife with sore humiliation fraught,
Or crowned with victory and love divine,—
　　What has it brought?

The day is dying in the west:
  What has it brought?
One day less distant from the waiting bliss;
  To endless rest
One day more near; to hand and brain o'erwrought,
What comforting is summed in this
  The day has brought?

THE WOODS IN EARLY SPRING.

I NEVER walk these woodland ways,
  And on the cast-off jewels tread,
Which crowned throughout the summer days,
  The naked boughs above my head,
Unless my pulses thrill and start
  At every footstep's slightest sound,
And I do feel within my heart,
  That it is consecrated ground.

Decay and ruin greet my eyes;
  Grim skeletons in silence stand;
Where all was life around me lies
  The work of death on every hand;

And every leaf beneath my feet,
  Which careless winds have thoughtless strown,
Marks where friend I was wont to greet,
  Or hides grave of friend I have known.

And yet I cannot think them dead,
  Though I behold Death's signals here;
Though from my vision they are fled,
  I know they must be somewhere near,
And have assumed these sombre hues,
  For purpose I cannot divine;
Or feint of death may be a ruse,
  Perchance, to test the faith of mine.

To every blackened arch and spire
  Clings something yet of former grace;
As mute strings of a broken lyre
  Recall outlines of some dear face,
Among these withered stems I see
  Familiar forms where'er I turn;
I breathe again, it seems to me,
  The spicy odor of the fern.

And even now, the while I look,
  Warm sunlight streaming through the boughs,

And into every hidden nook,
  With grace of life the germs endows,
Which only fragments of the dust
  Appeared to my half-blinded eyes;
And my heart swells with hope and trust,
  For I can see the dead arise.

AFTERWARDS.

No sky is so draped with thick clouds sweeping
    over,
  Obscuring and mocking the light of the sun,
But it will again its brightness recover,
  When the wrath of the storm is done.

No violet snatches from the blue bending over,
  So exquisite hue in the blossoming May,
But the litter of autumn the mould will cover,
  Where it withers and passes away.

No heart is so gay with frolic and laughter
  In its hours of abandon, most reckless and wild,
But the pang of some grief will come to it after,
  To which it is unreconciled.

No heart is so stricken and broken with sorrow,
　Overwhelming and crushing like death, to-day,
But there 'waits it some hopeful and brighter to-
　　morrow,
　When its woe shall have shrunken away.

The gray of no dawn is so winsome and tender,
　Heralding the fulness of beauty and light,
But the day rolls away, and its dying splendor
　Is chased by the shadows of night.

The gloom of no night is so long, and so cheerless,
　Though its measureless spaces seem infinite,
But the dawn of some morning will follow, as
　　peerless,
　As the suns before it have lit.

DISTANCE.

We always look too far away;
　　For aye,
More distant things attractive seem;
　　We dream

Of that beyond our reach and ken,
　　　　And then,
To gain it sacrifice that near
　　　　And dear.

We may think that the world is fair
　　　　Elsewhere,
And see not beauties that near by
　　　　Us lie;
Or sweetest harmonies may make
　　　　Awake
Some by-gone sorrow's mournful strain
　　　　Again.

The treasures our weak hands might clasp
　　　　We grasp
Not, or but half appreciate,
　　　　And wait,
Unsatisfied and hungering,
　　　　Something,
Which better through the veil of years
　　　　Appears.

Too far we seek our duty, too;
　　　　So do
Our efforts fail; close to our homes
　　　　It comes,

And needful opportunity,
      Maybe,
Awaits for us our very door
      Before.

We magnify that in our way
      To-day;
Fumes of suspicion's poison rise!
      Our eyes
Are blurred by them; to-morrow, though,
      Our foe
Disarms; and through its tinted dream
      Joys gleam.

Our wisdom classifies each star,
      Afar,
But gauges not some nearer light
      Aright;
Who sees how far an evil word
      Is heard,
Or counts steps love's dear feet have trod—
      But God!

TWO LIVES.

THE life of one men thought was almost blame-
    less :
        Ah! who can tell
What forces strove in him for mastery
Ere honor yielded up her citadel?
Among his fellows this one walked a king,
In wisdom, affluence, and everything
For which is longing, struggling, envying:
His magic touch wrought all successfully;
The voices of the world sang his renown;
Upon his brow love placed his regal crown:
        Ah! who can tell
        Why he went down?

The life of one was grovelling and aimless:
        Ah! who can know
The purposes that sway the human heart?
He lived and served and plodded; little, though,
By him the waters of life's sea were stirred:
Wealth crowned him not; fame whispered not a
    word;

Beyond a space his name was never heard;
Though steadfastly he played an humble part,
He could not climb, and reached to honors none;
And, at the end, seemed just where he begun:
> Ah! who can know
> What heights he won?

HOW LITTLE DO WE KNOW!

THEY tell us there are mountains in far Switzer-
land
Which send a dozen echoes back to those below;
Beyond the spaces by our narrow vision spanned
Are echoes God alone can understand:
> And what he hears, alas, how little do we
> know!

The sigh we breathe, the word we speak, the note
we sing,
> How little do we know how far some one will
> hear!
The kindly deed we do, the look of love we bring,
The soothing touch of our sweet comforting,
> How little do we know how some heart it will
> cheer!

The blow we strike, the wound we give, the heart
    we break,
  How little do we know our victim's suffering!
The loss we feel, the cross we bear, the blow we
    take,
The sacrifice for some dear one we make,
  How little do we know the strength that it will
    bring!

LOST.

I LOST a little seed, one day,
  And where I could not tell;
The careless wind took it away,
    And left it in God's care;
  Upon it then His sunshine fell,
And it was watered by His dew,
Till by and by a lily grew,
    And blossomed there.

A careless little word, one day,
  Out from my lips there fell,
And with my breath was blown away.
    What mortal it will greet,
  Or whither go, I cannot tell:

I hope it will not mischief do,
But will a lily grow into,
    With fragrance sweet.

I missed a little friend, one day,
    And tears like rain-drops fell,
And sorrow filled my heart alway,
    For he was much to me,
    And it is hard to say farewell;
But I would not have him again:
One of the King's own lilies, then,
    Were lost, maybe.

ACROSS THE FIELDS.

ACROSS the fields, across the fields,
    This bright October morn I pass;
The spiders' webs, like silver shields,
    Are hung upon the dripping grass;
Like mummies stand the mulleins sere,
    The sumach fires are flaming up,
And like a star of gold gleams here
    And there a late, lone buttercup.

Across the fields, across the fields,
   I catch kaleidoscopic views;
His wand again King Midas wields,
   And elm-tops turn to golden hues;
The glory of the autumn wood
   The sunset has a rival in;
The emeralds are dipped in blood,
   And revelries of death begin.

Across the fields, across the fields,
   The breath of distant snowflakes comes;
To it the grape his sweetness yields;
   A wailing song the wild bee hums;
And boys and girls, with cheeks of tan,
   The frosted leaves go tripping through,
The groves upon the hills to scan
   For treasures each year brings anew.

THEN EARTH WERE MORE LIKE HEAVEN.

IF more of men, in every land,
   Their brother men were truer to;
If fewer men would raise the hand
   To do what they ought not to do;

Were more controlled by power of love;
    Did fewer need restraint of fear,
More of the bliss of heaven above
    Life had within this lower sphere.

If rights of men were more the song,
    And self more hidden from the sight;
If men dared more oppose the wrong,
    And all cared more to live the right;
If deeds of love, not deeds of land,
    Seemed to mankind to be more dear,
Life were below more noble, grand,
    And earth to heaven would be more near.

If needs of men had greater claim,
    And sympathy more moved men's hearts;
Were lofty stations less the aim,
    And more would act well humbler parts;
If each more cheerfully would bear
    His burden up the hill of life,
More happiness on earth were there,
    And less of bitterness and strife.

Were colors true more kept in sight,
    And less concealed by cunning arts;

If secret thoughts, exposed to light,
  Showed less deceit in human hearts;
If less was feared the speech of men,
  And conscience taught more law and love,
Men, in this nether world, were then
  More worthy of the realms above.

And if a tempted brother fall,
  More would give hand of friendship still,
With willing mind forgetting all,
  And fewer push him down the hill;
If, through yet greater charity,
  The erring were by men forgiven,
Then more reclaimed from sin would be,
  And earth were more like unto heaven.

FRIENDSHIP.

WHEN from the path we go
    Is no retreat,
And cross and care and woe
    O'ercome complete:

To ease each little blow
    Drops on our feet,
Your loving aid we know,
    O Friendship sweet!

When not a shining ray
    Of hope is near,
And darker grows the way
    We grope in fear,
Your kindly strength will stay,
    Your light will cheer
The gloom of sorrow's sway,
    O Friendship dear!

THE BEST LEGACY.

An aged sire,—the story runs,—
    Believing dissolution near,
Called round his bed his weeping sons,
    That they his dying words might hear.

"Your father's lands," said he, "sell not;
    Concealed in them great treasure lies;
I know not where, but search each spot,
    Till coming time reveals the prize.

" Turn o'er the sod, and plough each field,
   And roll away each useless stone;
The source of wealth that lies concealed,
   Will surely be to you made known."

The dying father passed from earth;
   No hidden gold e'er did appear;
But his words proved of untold worth,—
   Rich harvests reaped the sons each year.

Rewards of industry are great;
   And self-earned bread has relish sweet
As daintier fare on costlier plate,
   Which pampered heirs of riches eat.

Who labors with an earnest hand
   In any chosen worthy field,
Lives for a purpose true and grand,
   Though fate does not him fortune yield.

Who gives his children gold or lands,
   Uncertain treasures to them leaves;
Who teaches them with willing hands
   To toil, best legacy bequeaths.

CLYDE.

O'ERWHELMED in grief was Maggie Brown,
　Sweet Maggie Brown—a bride—
A widow—just one year between—
　And darling baby Clyde.

Submitting meekly to her fate,
　She hid away the tears;
God gave her strength to struggle through
　Stern winter's hopes and fears.

Set free by genial breath of spring
　The streamlets sped along;
The merry robins came again
　And filled the air with song.

Again sprang up the violets,
　Earth bloomed again anew,
And every day the little Clyde
　To Maggie dearer grew,—

Too lovely grew to leave amidst
　Earth's bitterness and strife;
God took him from his mother's arms
　Into a better life.

A QUIET STREAM.

IT lies not underneath a southern sky,
Where gorgeous tropic splendor fills the eye,
And spicy winds must always whisper by.

It is no stream of some historic land,
Enriched with its rare old cathedrals grand,
Or painted by some mighty master's hand.

Our song is of a peaceful, happy vale,
Where stalwart arms and generous hearts prevail;
The simple beauties here we proudly hail.

We hail the freshness of the spring-time rain!
We hail the summer wild-flowers come again!
We hail the autumn's wealth of golden grain!

The clover-heads beneath the drifting snow
Shall hide; through leafless trees shall wildly blow
The rough December winds. What matter, though!

The hearth-fire glow shall mock the frost-king
    bold;
The winter's sport shall hide the winter's cold;
The joys exceed the woes a hundred-fold.

A quiet stream, still on and on it goes,
Between familiar wood-capped hills it flows,
And dearer to my heart each year it grows.

LABOR.

By artist's skill the canvas glows
    As love and taste design,
And landscape's hues or tints of rose
    Reflect his touch divine.

By sculptor's aid our fancy's dream
    Or forms endeared we hail,
And life and love and beauty gleam
    From marble cold and pale.

But by no magical decree
    The statue fair upsprings,
And blend in sweetest harmony
    The landscape's colorings.

One must serve long and patiently
   Who excellence achieves,
And fit to wear a crown must be
   Ere he the crown receives.

The gift of genius, rarest dower,
   What heights may it aspire !
Yet labor's arm unlocks its power,
   And lifts achievements higher.

THE DEATH OF THE CZAR.

THE great has fallen,—life has sped,—
A nation mourns its regal dead !
Judge not, O man ! He stands alone
Before the great, eternal throne :

And ye who glory in this hour,
And think o'erthrown despotic power,
Mistaken is your frenzied zeal ;
Red murder works no public weal.

Forget ye now his love and cheer
When bravest men grew pale with fear ?

When in that darkest night of all
Our nation grieved its leader's fall?

Although our hope and prophecy
Fulfilled we failed in him to see,
And we, on his historic page,
Read not the progress of the age:

The blow he struck for liberty
A score of million serfs made free.
Where in the world's heroic story
Are written deeds of greater glory?

So God be praised! Grudge not a tear,
Nor yet fling curses o'er his bier;
We mourn the sadness of his fall,
And ask God's mercy over all.

LOVE AND ART.

EARTH'S gems, art-touched, resplendent shine;
    The antique marble glows,
Wrought by a skill almost divine,
    And blooms with wreath and rose.

Each life is a mosaic grand,
   Mankind are artists all;
Yet, sometimes from an unknown hand
   The sweetest gems will fall.

For golden deeds not set in gold
   Some simple lives adorn,
And tales of love not ever told
   Put chivalry to scorn.

As gift of art makes beauty spring
   Up from a block of stone,
A loving heart makes man a king
   Without a crown or throne.

———

MATURITY.

As yields the peaceful night,
   With sweet and solemn stillness dumb,
When morning's rosy light
   Announces active day has come:

As yields the bud and leaf,
   And perfume sweet and blossom dear,
When come the fruit and sheaf,
   And wealth of autumn crowns the year:

So yields youth's gentler joy
   To stronger passion, braver hope,
When manhood crowns the boy,
   And brain and brawn have fullest scope.

BLACK EYES AND BLUE EYES.

A THRILLING power the black possess:
   They tell of brilliancy of mind,
Of depth of passion, restlessness,
   A soul to daring deeds inclined.
A tenderness lies in the blue:
   They speak a sympathizing heart,
Of friendship firm and true,
   And faithfulness, though distance part.

The black eye penetrates us through,
   And tremblingly it is obeyed;
So softly comes the glance of blue,
   Not knowing it, we're captives made.

We love the soul-lit eyes of blue,
    So calm, affectionate, content;
Admire the glowing, jetty hue,
    So sparkling, bright, magnificent.

BROTHERHOOD.

WHOE'ER thou art, thou art my brother:
    One taught it long ago;
And He said, "Love ye one another."
    If greater need one know
Than I do, Lord, let it be mine
    To whisper to him low,—
Brother, whate'er is mine is thine.

"Lift ye the burden of another"
    Is written, too, somewhere;
And if in sorrow is my brother,
    Some part is mine to bear;
Lord, help me, then, it to divine,
    That I may with him share,—
Brother, whate'er is thine is mine.

IN THE FIELDS.

Away from stately halls,
  From dusty streets away,
Out from the city's walls,
  I roam at will to-day.

On me your hottest ray,
  O summer sun, let down;
I breathe pure air to-day,
  Though my pale cheeks grow brown.

I walk through fields of gold,
  And gather jewels bright;
The wealth cannot be told
  Of treasures greet my sight.

Upon the side-hill there—
  Whoever knew such luck?—
Raspberries ripe and fair
  With eagerness I pluck.

Young wintergreens I pull
   Along my rambling way,
And fill my pockets full,—
   I am a boy to-day.

Beside the brook I stroll
   That winds along the vale,
Whose waters, as they roll,
   Tell me a pleasing tale.

Among the sweet wild-flowers
   That bloom beside the stream,
How swiftly pass the hours!
   How very brief they seem!

So, climbing up the hills
   And wandering through the vales,
My heart with gladness fills;
   But human strength soon fails.

Now prostrate on the ground
   My weary limbs I fling,
And pleasant rest is found
   Beside a bubbling spring.

I dream, O God, of Thee,
   The generous gifts of thine:
What blessings are for me!
   What priceless riches mine!

The gentle winds blow free,
   Shine free the stars above;
Beneath and over me
   All things proclaim His love.

I thank him for the flowers
   And for the evening dew,
And for the sun and showers
   Which make earth bloom anew.

O Nature, if with thee
   I could commune yet more,
Content would dwell with me
   And fill me o'er and o'er.

AFTER THE STORM.

DEEP slumber's peace kind Heaven to me brought;
Yet while I slept a miracle was wrought.
  The curtains of the sky uprolled, and, lo!
  Paling the starlight's glow,
  A harvest fell—of snow;
  And hands unseen rolled many a long windrow
In the wild night, white-capping hedge and wall,
And far as eye can see is spotless all.

An opal sky rests on the ermined hill;
The maple's boughs white coral clusters fill;
  The pine-tree's hanging cones pale taper fingers
     seem;
  And in the sunlight's beam,
  Like costly jewels, gleam
  The alder's crystals o'er the frozen stream:
White plumes the elm's high branches wave and
     dip,
And icy beads the tiny pear-twigs tip.

All hushed is now the night's wild minstrelsy;
The stillness only breaks the chickadee,

Whose warm, brave heart no biting cold can
    chill.
I listen to his trill;
With joy my senses thrill;
Into God's presence I come closer still;
And in my heart the longing springs and grows
To be more like the landscape's stainless snows.

IN OCTOBER DAYS.

FROM the maple's mottled cloak,
From the elm, and from the oak,
One by one come flying down
Leaves of crimson, gold and brown;
Milk-weed bursts its conic pod;
Dimmer grows the golden-rod;
Hazels ripen in the copse;
Mountain-ashes' berried tops,
And the budded sumachs blaze
      In October days.

Down of thistles wildly flies,
Frosted vine on trellis dies;

Mystic sheets of filmy lace
Dewy mornings meadows grace;
Sere sunflowers and hollyhocks
Slant along the garden walks;
Gentians linger blue and fair,
Ox-eyes glimmer here and there;
Sunlight mellows through the haze
  In October days.

Dodging out of sight and reach,
Squirrels haunt the fruity beech;
Weasels steal along the wold
To the crib or chicken-fold;
Sleek and fat the partridge drums;
Now and then a wild bee hums;
Winging round the hemlock high,
Crows in chorus hoarsely cry;
Crickets sing shrill roundelays
  In October days.

Lustrous apples, red and white,
Cater to the appetite;
Pressed from cheese of pomace brown,
Liquid amber gurgles down,

Throbbing pulses quicker yet
With a nectar none forget;
Pumpkins shine as golden rocks
Rolled between ripe, lusty shocks
Of the sickled, glassy maize
          In October days.

Nights are longer, evenings cold;
Chestnut-burs relax their hold;
Noisy mills part grain and chaff,
Burly threshers joke and laugh;
Lovers creep within the door,
Softly breathing nothings o'er;
So, with hues of dying things,
Wine of life distils and brings
Blessings to us many ways
          In October days.

FAREWELL TO SUMMER.

SWEETHEART, when first I looked on thee so flush
    With thy unfolding tender blades of green,
So lavish of thy bursting rosebud's blush,
    Thy violets and all thy dainty sheen,

I loved thee, then, sweetheart, ah, me!
And all my heart went out to thee.

And when the fulness of thy bloom so soon
   Brought with it drowsy hum of roving bees,
And bearding wheat, and sultry, melting noon,
   And breezes waving white and crimson seas,
I loved thee, then, sweetheart, ah, me!
And all my being thrilled with thee.

And in the crowning glory of thy days,
   When harvests manifold attest thy worth,
And woods in dying splendor briefly blaze
   Ere sombre shadows fall on all the earth,
I love thee, too, sweetheart, ah, me!
And grieve to say good-by to thee.

PRIESTS.

Amid the gloom of the wild and moonless night,
   As the stars gleam fitfully,
   Long lines of maples I see,
And their leafless boughs with fleecy flakes are
     white.

Tall priests in their gowns they seem, and the
　　　winds that blow
　　And sway them are litanies
　　That are whispered in services
Over summer's bloom at their feet dead under the
　　snow.

CORN.

THE August winds are holding on the lea—
　　With scarce a lull between—
Their roughest carnival of revelry.
Broad blades and tasselled spears sway mightily,
　　And from afar is seen
　　The splendor of their sheen.
I look on rolling waves, it seems to me,
But marvel at the strangeness of a sea
　　Whose billows' crests are green.

OASES.

LARGE fruitful fields, with beauty rare,
Of living green, are sometimes where
　　For most part barren sands abound :

So in life's endless round and wear
Of crushing toil and grinding care
  Are pleasant resting-places found.
Dear are the social joys we share,
Sweet is the breath of blossoms fair
  Which strew beneath our feet the ground :
Kind friends help us our burdens bear,
And deeds of love beyond compare,
  Our darkest hours with light surround.

Yet in the desert all is barren waste
  Save some few oases of green,
While life is all with love and beauty graced,
  Save where some barren spots are seen.

BEYOND.

THE angry wind passes by
  To some realm that farther lies;
And the roar we tremble at,
  Beyond in the distance dies.

Beyond the shallowest brook
  That laughingly goes its way,
Rolls the river's flood; beyond
  It is ocean's foam and spray.

Beyond the bare boughs is bloom;
   Beyond the blossom's decay
The sweet mellow fruit matures,
   And gladdens many a day.

Beyond the cloud and the storm
   Streams of sunlight flood the skies;
The day lies beyond the night,
   In the dawn the darkness dies.

Restless day leaps on, and in
   The flush of the sunset sinks;
Swift years glide to years beyond,
   And end as never one thinks.

JUNE.

So thou art here again, my queen,
With puffs and frills and dainty sheen,
And young as ever thou hast been
   Since I remember first thy coming;
Yet every bit as old as I
Thou wert in days long since gone by,
When I chased thy pale butterfly,
   And marvelled at thy wild bee's humming.

But while I have grown stiff and gray
In years that have slipped fast away,
With children thou dost romp and play
   As if thou knewest not of grieving,
And had'st not known a single care;
And now thou comest, blithe and fair,
With lilac blossoms in thy hair,
   Along thy pathway perfume leaving.

The delicatest buds unfold,
And when they look on thee grow bold;
The dandelion gives its gold
   To don a cap of lace and feather;
The mustards lose their yellow hair,
The locusts hang out opals rare,
Their pink-white gowns azaleas wear,
   Fearing naught of thy gentle weather.

Fair queen, tell me, in very truth,
What is the secret of thy youth?
Whence comes the power of thine? Forsooth,
   Thy ways are all past my discerning;
I think thou art a witch, maybe,
Who by some weird necromancy
Has charmed each blade and leaf and tree,
   And they leap out at thy returning.

Or, art thou, too, a slave, as I,
Who in thy niche of space must lie
As one by one the months go by?
   The very flowers thy hand upreareth,
When thou art helpless to give aid,
Midsummer's sun shall scorch and fade,
And death shall blacken wold and glade
   Before thy bloom again appeareth.

IN EXTREMIS.

A NATION's hero, stricken, dying lies,
     And many eyes
Throughout the land which owes so much to him,
     With tears are dim.

Through fire and death he led our brave men on
     To victory won,
Yet now with resignation waits before
     Death's open door.

While story's page our mournful past unfolds,
     Or legend holds,
Forgotten will not be his help to save,
     Or blows he gave.

He, whom no higher honors life can give,
    In death will live;
And while heroic deeds lift men to fame,
    Will glow his name.

And generations yet unborn will come
    Seeking his tomb,
And proudly o'er his dust do homage due
    One great and true.

LIGHT AND LOVE.

Sin and sorrow shadowing the day,
Night and error leading us astray,
Light and love enfolding us alway;
Hail the sunlight flaming through the darkness
    riven!
Hail the love-light overflowing earth and heaven;

SERVITUDE.

Who lives a life of bondage, yet may have
    Some hours of respite from servility;
Who cannot rule himself, he is a slave
    Who cannot once escape his master's eye.

VANITY.

A miser—and often charity
Half of her sweetness yields to his insatiate greed;
    An ass whose ears persistently
Protruding mar the grandeur of many a noble deed.

AT LAST.

Backward rolling never,
    Freighted with our toil and tears,
Shorter growing ever,
    Onward swiftly go the years;

Hoping, trusting, now we mount,
    Failing, faithless, now we fall ;
Yet some good God's final count,
    In our lives may trace through all.

THOUGHT.

Who yet sees those that he loves best,
    However far from him away,
With their sweet comforting is blest,
    And friends surround him every day.

While he, who those he thinks his foes,
    Keeps constantly before his eyes,
However far from them he goes,
    Lives always with his enemies.

A BREEZE OF JUNE.

A BREEZE of June,
  With whistle and croon,
Up and down the valley,
  I creep through the grasses,
To frolic and dally
  With the lithe meadow lasses.

Over hill and hollow,
  I tickle and tease them,
And they try to follow
  Me ; it seems to please them.

Stately and tall,
  High-born and low,
I jostle them all,
  And they reel to and fro.

On their slender rods,
  I buttercups sway,
And the daisy nods,
  If I touch her, alway.

Red-top and clover
  With me waltz and chassez,
And the lily bends over
  Like a drunken fay.

Soft and low I speak,
  Or I rave and scold;
Each turns me her cheek,
  Which is fairer than gold.

How pretty their gowns!
  How charming their graces!
But they tumble like clowns
  When I breathe on their faces.

The heads of the barley
  I rock till they quiver
And roll on the far lea
  Like the waves of the river.

Unharmed I stride
  Over spears at my feet,
And with poppies play hide
  And seek in the wheat.

From blossom and vine
I drink off the dew,
Delicious as kisses,
Bewitching as wine,
Without measure or stint;
And never one misses
The fragrance with which I fill
Of violet, daffodil,
Fern and balm and mint
And mallow and rue,
Till I cannot tell
Which the sweeter be,
Spice of pimpernel
Or fleur-de-lis.

Every foolish lass
Flutters so when I pass,—
It is easy to see that I move her;
And each believes me her lover,
Devoted and true.
When I am gone, I know
They will pine for me so;
Maybe will sigh
And wither and die;

But what can I do,
Or what care I,
As I frolic and croon,
A breeze of June?

UNPLEASANT THINGS.

OH, life is dear through all its tangled mazes:
Full many pleasing legends tell
Of those who in Arcadia dwell;
    Life's fairer phases
The poet's glowing numbers swell
    In endless praises:
But seldom is there one who sings
The graces of unpleasant things.

Oh, it is sweet in that dear vale to wander,
    Where yesterday's fair waters flow,
    Where blossoms of remembrance blow,
        And there to ponder
O'er treasured flowers that brighter glow
        As we grow fonder:
But is there one who fondly clings
To memories of unpleasant things?

Oh, bright is that dear land of our fair fancy's
    Ken, with warm skies and cool grottos!
Down waveless streams in safe bateaux
    One there advances;
The splendor of its famed châteaux
    The heart entrances:
But from that dreamy land who brings
Back glimpses of unpleasant things?

Oh, in that realm where always up is springing
    That dear old song forever sung,
With countless changes sweetly rung,
    And always ringing,—
Which, ever old and always young,
    Hearts will be singing
While Love his golden arrows flings,
Oh, are there there unpleasant things?

Oh, in our age and since the world's beginning,
    Around sweet song fond hearts entwine,
And men bow down before its shrine,
    Nor think it sinning
To call the harmony divine
    Which is so winning:
But on its harps of many strings
Who cares to play unpleasant things?

Oh, dear and fair and many are the treasures
    To restless, seeking mortals come,
    As over sea and land they roam ;
       Yet sweetest pleasures
    Are in that place we call our home,
       In fullest measures :
    But where our joy the purest springs,
    Why need there be unpleasant things ?

Oh, all along through years of centuries hoary,
    From pulpit down to pew has rolled,
    From lips of parsons, wise and bold,
       That dear old story,
    So much to us, so sweetly told,
       Of coming glory :
    At last, perhaps, the preacher rings
    The changes on unpleasant things.

Oh, wealth ! we learn thy value to our sorrow
    In all the things around we see,
    Denied because of poverty,
       In that we borrow
    To-day, and think and hope that we
       May pay to-morrow :
    But is there one who never wrings
    Good money from unpleasant things?

Oh, in the stories of heroic ages,
  How men have worshipped heroes' shrines!
  The splendor of great kingdoms shines
   In many pages,
  Through fascinating glowing lines
   Of toiling sages:
  But in those records of great kings,
  What pictures of unpleasant things!

Oh, when by mortal ken the clouds are riven,
  Beyond which lies the gold we quest—
  That fairest land of dearest rest—
   In that dear heaven,
  To an expected, welcome guest,
   With all forgiven,
  Oh, will there evermore be stings
  Of earthly, sad, unpleasant things?

Oh, warp and weft of toil make life successful,
  And burning heat its gold refines;
  Of bitter grapes, that yield sweet wines,
   This life it is full;
  Through pain of death the glory shines
   Of life more blissful:
  Oh, higher up we mount on wings
  Of blessings in unpleasant things.

TRANSMUTATION.

I LOOK out on a wintry sky :
The feathered tree-tops snap and break,
The leas are all with crystals walled,
Whose dazzling lustre blinds my eyes ;
Oh, mystery of mysteries,
That fills my soul with ecstasy !
I look out on the sky again,
And, where the cold, white snow had lain,
Some wizard's hand has touched each flake,
And wrought of it an emerald.

FOR HER ALONE.

OH, not for him, so cold and pallid there,
    Who lies in peaceful sleep ;
All know that he was pure and brave and fair ;
    Oh, not for him I weep.

But her bereft of all she has to give,
All losses merged in one,
Who, hopeless, helpless, dead, yet still must live,
I weep for her alone.

THE NATION'S DEAD.

THE bird is no longer singing,
But the song is still in the air;
To the thistle no bloom is clinging,
But the down floats here and there.

The buds and the blossoms wither,
But the fragrance is everywhere;
The dead leaves blow yon and hither,
But the fruit is ripe and fair.

The willows above them are bending,
But the end of their days is not;
Their lives and our lives are blending,
Though the peace of death is their lot.

OLD AND NEW.

OLD Year, thou hast our joys to sorrows wed;
Thou art the tomb of aspirations dead
And ruined hopes; thy hour has come at last!
We give thee up to the unmeasured past.

Thy blasting touch has left on beauty's brow
Traces that ineffaceable are now.
Fair hair has whitened in thy bleaching breath;
Thy footsteps have been harbingers of death;
Friends crowned with years have tottered to the
        tomb,
And those we loved have withered in their bloom.

Now, as upon the threshold of the New,
With buoyant hope we bid the Old adieu,
What memories come thronging through the brain!
What spectres from the past rise up again;
What ghosts of broken vows and trusts betrayed!
How unfulfilled are prophecies we made;
How much we planned; how little we achieved;
Where we expected most, the most deceived;

How little good in all we wrought appears!
But so the story is of countless years;
Men climb to greatness, glory fades away;
They build up cloud-capped towers, but they
  decay;
And men, where naught remains of monarchies,
Once trembled at imperial decrees.

The wondrous plans of God none understand;
It may be, though we strive with faithful hand
And find ambition's goal beyond us lies,
Our conscientious toil still fructifies;
Success sometimes leads to oblivion down,
While seeming failure wears immortal crown.

Thy course is run, Old Year. Good-by to thee!
Hope greets the New: we seek its mystery
Expectant, glad; a monument sublime
Is human faith in every age and clime;
Though years bring to us neither peace nor power,
Sweet, trusting faith can brighten every hour;
So, God be praised! thou dear old friend, adieu!
And hail, all hail the coming of the New!

FATE.

UNANSWERED seemingly your many prayers?
　Denied so many things for which you long?
　So grievous is the burden of some wrong,
Some sorrow that steals on you unawares?
　　Oh, in the anguish of your woe,
　　Fate may be kinder than you know.

Unanswered prayer may save from wretchedness;
　Diviner strength denial may lead to;
　To bear a wrong is less than one to do;
Sorrow to One who leaves none comfortless
　　May bring you; so do sufferings
　　Lift men sometimes to better things.

MIRRORS.

Two fabled beasts, in days of old,
　'Tis said, had each a looking-glass,
Wherein each saw himself a bold,
　Fierce lion crouched where none could pass.

But it so chanced, upon a time,
　　That each looked in the other's glass;
And, lo! each saw, with wrath sublime,
　　Himself reflected as an ass.

As in that age, it is in this,
　　Our mirrors flatter us, alas!
Who sees himself just as he is,
　　Must look into another's glass.

And he does best who learns to know
　　Himself seen through another's eyes;
His weaknesses to him they show,
　　And strengthen him and make him wise.

WHY LINGER SO?

A GOLDEN sheen
　　Is on the willows;
Bright threads of green
　　Fringe all the meadows.
The sparrow twitters,
　　Warm breezes blow,
Oh, tardy blossoms,
　　Why linger so?

The noisy rills
  Leap down the gullies;
Behind the hills
  And in the hollows
The sunbeam's kisses
  Lap up the snow;
Oh, tardy blossoms,
  Why linger so?

I hear the song
  Again of bluebird,
The boughs among
  Of elm and maple;
With maiden-blushes
  The young buds glow;
Oh, tardy blossoms,
  Why linger so?

The green frogs peep
  In spongy lowlands;
The swallows sweep
  Around the gables;
Impatiently, for
  The lilacs, though,
The bees are waiting;
  Why linger so?

7

LEAF AND DROP.

A TINY drop, in dusky starlight,
    With a rose-leaf lover lay,
But a sun-ray from the far height,
    Warming up the growing day,
Lured her from a bed of sweetness
    Into morning mist again,—
So a picture goes with fleetness
    From the frosted window-pane.

Came this guest for love or duty?
    Let the wooing rose-leaf tell;
Tell it by the lustrous beauty,
    Where the crystal kisses fell;
Or, if morning perfume-laden,
    Thrills with sweetness, freshness, grace;
Surely, then, thy beauty, maiden,
    Tells of drop and leaf's embrace.

BETTER TO-DAY THAN YESTER-
DAY.

MOURN not, my brother, forever over
  The losses and crosses of yesterday;
Opportunities gone you cannot recover,
  If you sigh and sorrow for them alway;
Wisdom is not, my brother, in grieving;
  Far wiser it is to endeavor to say,
When the night comes on, yourself not deceiving,
  I am better to-day than yesterday.

I will sin to-day and do better to-morrow,
  Is unwise, my brother, though easy to say;
For, it is pledging the future to borrow
  What we shall never have strength to pay;
Though sweet is the voice of pleasure calling,
  It is sweeter yet to be able to say,
When the day is spent and the shadows are falling,
  I am better to-day than yesterday.

If one of us stumbles, some day, my brother,
  And falls, oh, pass him not by,—not yet;
He lifts himself who raises another,
  And the service God will not forget;

And let it forgotten, my brother, be never,
   That for each of us it is hard to say,
Though striving to be vigilant ever,
   I am better to-day than yesterday.

A king the ideal to-morrow anoints us,
Disrobes and discrowns us the real to-day;
   Wherever, my brother, God's finger points us,
There is something for us to do alway;
   Though often we fail, if ever essaying,
At night's oncoming, my brother, we may,
   At last, with joy, be truthfully saying,
I am better to-day than yesterday.

CONCEIT.

Oh, witch, Conceit! Oh, cunning elf!
   Against thee who can lock the door?
For no man sees thee in himself,
   Yet in another all abhor;
In presence of thy flaunting shame
   Wisdom and modest worth retreat;
Oh, thou repulsive, hated name,
   Opinionated hag, Conceit!

THE CLOCK.

ITs lazy pendulum does mark
   For us youth's lagging hours so slow,
   That we grieve that we do not know
How we may shorten up its arc.

In after years, how glad were we,
   Alas! to stay its pendulum;
   So fast the measured strokes do come,
And crowd on us our destiny.

OUR BEST.

NOT what we do or do not glean;
Not in what fields we toil, I ween;
Not even to what heights we climb
In these few years that mark off time.

To act out well one humble part,
And keep love yet within the heart,
As days and months and years go by,
And we grow old and fail and die.

7*

Each day to feel we do the best
We can, will give us peace and rest;
And who attains most happiness
Does nothing more, does nothing less.

FROST.

WHERE grass-spires grew and nodded
With every wind that blew,
Long days of summer through,
Snow-drifts are on the leas,
And not a leaf or blossom
Is on the apple-trees.

But last night while I dreaming
Lay, stem and leaf and vine,
Of every known design,
Surely came back again;
Or else their pallid ghosts are
Haunting my window-pane.

PALMISTRY.

ONE looked on the face of a withered crone,
In the palm of a dimpled hand looked one.

Black eyes of one of them pierced you through,
Then the eyes of one, the skies were less blue.

One's feet trod buttercups yellow as gold,
The forehead of one was wrinkled and old.

"Oh, when shall I wed?" one asked with glee.
"A sweet, pale face," one answered, "I see."

"Oh, will my lover be true?" one said.
"I see," said the crone, "a maiden,—dead."

DRIFTING.

ALONE and adrift I lie in my boat,
  With my face upturned to the cloudless sky ;
And on and on I lazily float
  On the crests of the billows, rolling high.

The far-away voice of a crow loudly calls,
   As his outstretched wings cleave the azure air;
While over my face the sunlight falls,
   The wind cools my forehead and plays with my
      hair.

Above, the measureless blue of the skies;
   Beneath, the blue-green waters are deep;
I listen and dream, and I close my eyes,
   And in utter abandon I rest and sleep.

In the peace of forgetfulness so sweet,
   Unburdened of all life's sorrows I float,
As the white-capped waves roll under my feet,
   And adrift and alone I lie in my boat.

LOVE'S PLAINT AND PRAYER.

TOGETHER have the currents of our lives
   Uninterruptedly and calmly flowed
      Along;
Quick as a bolt of lightning rives
      The strong
   Oak, can love now be overthrowed?

And must the pathways lead henceforth apart,
  Of those whose love unto such magnitude
    Has grown,
That unto each the other's heart
    Is known,
  And every throb is understood?

And what the mighty force can overcome,
  Resistless, overwhelming passion's power,
    Whose height
And depth to speak the lips are dumb;
    Whose light
  Illumes and charms night's darkest hour?

Can lightning's flame consume, or fire devour
  That which of flame is born, on fire is fed?
    What thought
Of death, to make love fear has power,
    When naught
  Is death but life, if love is dead?

Though love through sorrow leads and suffering,
  Can woe unloose the chains that love has bound?
    Resign

To pain, shall love his throne? A king
    Divine
  Is love in tribulation found.

Oh, that is but the counterfeited thing
  Which measures and divides and calculates
    Its hold;
Great passion is not bound by ring
    Of gold,
  Is kindled not by grand estates.

Think you, if love had gift of prophecy,
  And all things unto its prophetic eyes
    Were shown,
And all the heartaches sure to be
    Were known,
  That it would shrink in anywise?

We reach the height of passion's power supreme
  But through the heart's supremest agony;
    And when
The heart may crushed and breaking seem,
    Pain then
  Becomes divinest ecstasy,

If through it a more perfect love we know ;
   To live, to die, to serve and hope and wait,—
      In all
To share whate'er of weal or woe
      Befall,—
Love seeks and asks no better fate.

SUMMER RAIN.

Oh, summer rain ! glad summer rain !
When corn-blades writhe as if in pain,
   And leaf and blossom everywhere
Are withering in the sun's hot ray ;
   When drifting dust fills all the air,
And clouds that sweep along the way
Turn golden-rod and asters gray,—
   Oh, welcome, summer rain !

Oh, summer rain ! sweet summer rain !
When lowing cattle seek in vain
   For well-known pool to slake their thirst,
And in the brooklet's stony bed
   Find scarcely once a draught, where erst

By banks now brown with grasses dead,
So boisterously the waters sped,—
   Oh, welcome, summer rain!

Oh, summer rain! fair summer rain!
To those who cross the distant plain
   Away from fertile fields and streams;
Where barren deserts scorch and blaze,
   And thirst a fire consuming seems,
As wearily drag out the days
Beneath the blistering tropic rays,—
   Oh, welcome, summer rain!

Oh, summer rain! kind summer rain!
When one we love has wasting lain
   On weary bed, with fever burned;
And scarce we mark the pulse's beats,
   And on each throb our hope is turned,
As through the lattice's parted cleats,
The cooler breath the sick one greets,—
   Oh, welcome, summer rain!

Oh, summer rain! cool summer rain!
When slowly rolls the squeaking wain
   Through all the lengthened, melting day,
As jaded steeds, with gall and smart,
   Creep on along the dust-clogged way,

And tire and felloe fall apart,
Defying the mechanic's art,—
    Oh, welcome, summer rain!

Oh, summer rain, free summer rain!
What blessings follow in its train!
    O'erhead and underneath our feet,
All living things are beautified;
    The stifling air grows cool and sweet,
And vision reaching far and wide,
Greets miracles on every side,
    Wrought by the summer rain.

Oh, summer rain! pure summer rain!
From lily's robe is washed the stain;
    The scarlet poppies brighter glow;
Brown bumblebees, with new delight,
    Delve in the thistle's purple blow;
And lustre of the circling white
Rays of the daisies dims the sight,—
    Oh, welcome, summer rain!

Oh, summer rain! rich summer rain!
When fruitful months go by again,
    And yellow sheaf and ripened ear

8

Are garnered in the plethoric bin,
 And winter comes all lean and sere;
For all the treasures gathered in,
For all our toil has helped to win,
 We bless the summer rain.

WHEN I AM DEAD.

WHEN I am dead:
And dark earth hides me from the sight of men,
 Strew only flowers above my head,
That you would bring me were I living then.

When I am dead:
No words let your lips speak of me in praise
 Because the living spark has fled
But you would say of me were true always.

When I am dead:
What I have sinned, what wrong have done to
  men,
 Curse me not for, nor seek, instead,
To turn my vices into virtues then.

When I am dead :
Carve on my stone, nor word, nor line, nor verse,
But they who knew me must have said,
It were like him,—no better and no worse.

When I am dead :
As if I were yet of you, speak of me ;
These scenes sometimes, revisited,
Will seem like old times, then, if it may be.

RESIGNATION.

OURSELVES we are unfaithful to :
We waste strength in complaints and sighs,
Nor find the best that in us lies,
Achieving not what we might do
With common things before our eyes.

It seems so hard for us to know
The measure of our happiness
Is rightly gauged, or more or less,
Not by the grapes around us grow,
But by the wine from them we press.

If we could have what we have not,
　　Or look up to some fairer skies,
　　We think, or we had wings to rise
Above conditions of our lot,
　　That we should find our paradise.

It is for us the world to take
　　Just as we find it here and there,
　　And with the pittance of our share
Of its imperfect things, to make
　　Each day a blessing rich and fair.

Our problem is, what is to use,
　　And what may be, from it divine;
　　The humblest gift the fates consign,
It is not wisdom to refuse
　　Because for something else we pine.

The harvest shall come by and by
　　To him who leaves behind the wailing crowd;
　　What matters if thick darkness shroud,
Or mists shall gather in the sky,
　　The blue is e'er above the cloud.

ONE AFTERNOON.

THE poppies on their stems did hardly sway;
  The ripening June grass showed a purple tinge;
    The wide lagoon
Far to the east in glowing beauty lay;
  Upon the western sky hung rosy fringe,
    One afternoon.

Eye dazzled with the lustre of the leas;
  Ear but the harmony of silence heard;
    The winds their croon
Had hushed, and scarce a leaf upon the trees,
  Although with their full glory crowned, was
      stirred,
    One afternoon.

A dream of Paradise the wheat-lands lay;
  Earth's warring elements were sunken in
    A death-like swoon,
O'ercome by sweetness of the perfect day,
  And far away seemed bitterness and sin,
    One afternoon.

Girt with a silken sash around the waist,
  Adown the green and crimson aisles one came
    With noiseless shoon,
Whom all the bluebirds seemed to know, and haste
  To greet with song, and with her kinship claim,
    One afternoon.

The waning day in throes of splendor died,
  And gathered on the primrose leaves the dew;
    But the faint moon
Her crescent hung above, no place beside
  One-half so fair,—so dear the meadow grew,
    One afternoon.

I cannot tell the thoughts that burned my brain,
  Nor sing the melody that filled my soul
    With rapture soon;
And only know divinest art were vain
  E'er to express joy to my heart that stole
    One afternoon.

NATURE'S JEWELS.

WROUGHT out of emerald, the quaint designs,
  In blade and leaf and frond, she first displays;
In amethyst and opal she outlines
  Them on the blossoms of the summer days;
In ruby tints and gold they glow again,
  When breath of autumn field and wood sweeps
    o'er;
On winter nights, upon the window-pane,
  In silver they are pictured out once more.

AN IDYL OF THE SPRING.

POETRY is everywhere:
  Stand beside the bubbling spring,
  Hearken to the whispering
Of the rhythmic voices there.

Hear the tender melodies
  Piped upon the slender reeds;
  Watch the wingèd thistle-seeds
Flying upward to the skies.

See the pendent laces cling
  To the rough projecting rocks;
  Maybe fallen from the frocks
Of the Naiads loitering.

See that supple, writhing form
  Far out on the reaching stone,
  Spying out a world unknown,
Hero-like, though but a worm.

Do you catch the glint of wings,
  Or the war-cry of the bee
  Pilfering the raspberry
That out o'er the water swings?

Here are spire and arch and line,
  Every form of perfect grace
  Crowded in this narrow space,
Fashioned but with skill divine.

By the zephyr tossed and whirled,
  Here are myriad forms of life;
  Here is all the mimic strife
Of a little bustling world.

HUSKS.

THE serried rank and file I walked among;
  The broad, thick blades above my shoulders
      spread;
To every waist a silken girdle hung,
  While countless mottled plumes waved o'er my
      head.
    Men prophesied rich harvesting
    In autumn days my field would bring;
    But, oh, the cruel mockery!
    To find where many an ear should be
      Nothing but husks.

So I have looked upon the forms of men
  By nature fashioned for some mighty end,
Whose vision ranged beyond the common ken,
  Whom every Christian grace seemed to befriend;
    And I have said, These lives, behold!
    A precious harvest will unfold;
    But, oh, the cruel mockery!
    To find where some good fruit should be
      Nothing but husks.

FOREVER.

WHOEVER smites the wrong, the right upholding
   In spite of error's clamoring cries;
Whoe'er uproots the false, the truth unfolding
   Along the paths where ignorance lies;
Whoe'er opposes vice is nobly giving
   To virtue's cause his best endeavor;
However lowly life he lives, is living
   A life to be forgotten never.

Whoever lifts his hand against oppression,
   Where'er the blighting curse may fall;
Whoever makes his life a sweet expression
   Of love, of equal rights for all;
Whoe'er the work of hand or brain bestowing
   Assists the tyrant's chains to sever;
Though humble deeds he does, some seed is sowing,
   Whose fruit will gladden hearts forever.

Whoe'er to an afflicted brother, needing,
   Extends the hand of charity;
Whoe'er binds up a heart that's broken, bleeding,
   With bonds of love and sympathy;

Whoe'er by kindly word or act bestowing,
  Binds hearts of men more close together;
His deeds, through rolling years, in beauty growing,
  Shall live in memory forever.

Whoe'er from sin and shame and degradation
  Assists an erring one to rise;
Whoe'er with life itself upholds the nation
  If freedom needs the sacrifice;
Whoe'er lives not for selfish ends and glory,
  The law of love forgetting never;
His name, though written not in song and story,
  Will live in human hearts forever.

SNOW-FLAKES.

MAYBE these myriad crystals in the air,
That linger on my face and in my hair,
And throw a misty veil across the skies,
Are winged particles of the chilled song
Of merry birds that used to greet my eyes;
Whose mellow notes were echoed everywhere
Before these sunless days and nights, so long,
Had frozen up their liquid melodies.

Maybe, for all their seeming artlessness,
Next summer's secrets they might now confess;
That peach and lilac's graces in them lie
Concealed, and only wait the charm of May
To quicken into bloom with her caress.
When, lo! a miracle, the world will cry,
For every spot where once a white flake lay,
Will lift some blade or blossom towards the sky.

Maybe a message on their unseen wings
Is borne—if I could understand all things—
From some dear one that now I know no more,
Although once of my very life a part;
Who yet remembers on some distant shore
Beyond the range of mortal ears, and sings
To soothe the anguish of my stricken heart,
And wake again sweet memories of yore.

Maybe these forms of innocence and grace
The storm whirls wildly now against my face,
In that pure land from this so far away
My angel sister's stainless lips have kissed,
And at her bidding cleave the realms of space,
Themselves the masters of the winds that play
With them, and seem to drive them where they list:
Ah! who can tell whose messengers are they?

APART.

A RIVULET runs at my feet,—
  How still its water glides;
But these high banks can never meet
  Which this small stream divides.

A word,—a little thing, I wis,—
  That easily is said;
But spoken once, how strange is this
  Love afterwards is dead!

SONG OF THE WIND.

I BLOW, blow, blow!
For I am the wind; from afar I come
  With bluster and might and speed;
    The crystals of snow,
  As I toss the thistle-seed,
I whirl and carry with me as I roam,
    And blow, blow, blow.

I crash, crash, crash!
For I am the wind; and the mocking trees
That stand along my way
I lash, lash, lash;
Their branches I snap and sway,
Or their trunks I shiver and break as I please,
And crash, crash, crash.

I sweep, sweep, sweep
Over the dark and limitless sea;
As the face of the waters I kiss,
They leap, leap, leap;
Their writhing to me is bliss;
As they foam and seethe in their agony,
I sweep, sweep, sweep.

I blow, blow, blow
On the sail spread out to catch my breeze,
And the canvas full I fill
For weal or woe;
The ship is rocked at my will,
As around and beneath it I swell the seas,
And blow, blow, blow.

I roar, roar, roar,
And it echoes on the mountain height;
  Valley and prairie wide
    I litter o'er;
The castles, men build in their pride,
I turn upon in my fury, and smite,
      And roar, roar, roar.

      I rave, rave, rave,
And destroy, yet blessings I carry, too;
  While I make men tremble with fear,
    I save, save, save
From many a pestilence near;
To cleanse the air and sweeten the dew,
    I rave, rave, rave.

      I break, break, break
With my startling cadences on the ear;
  Through the door I follow each guest,
      And take, take, take
Of the feast a scent of the best;
Through bars and bolts unseen, without fear,
      I break, break, break.

I pass, pass, pass
Over the violet's bended head;
At my lightest touch quivereth
The slender grass;
While the daisy sways with my breath,
And the clover shrinks from my tread,
I pass, pass, pass.

I drink, drink, drink
From fountain and river on my way,
And I drape the sky with the cloud;
I sink, sink, sink
It with flash and with thunder loud
To the earth, and its thirst the waters allay
I drink, drink, drink.

NOVEMBER.

SHE wears a scanty, fretted gown,
And all her garb is dingy brown,
She carries on her face a frown,
And always seems so grave and sober;

No flashing fire leaps from her eyes,
And woodlands gold and scarlet dyes;
No gaudy banners on the skies
    She hangs, as did our lost October.

Grass-blades grow stiff beneath her feet,
And herds find them no longer sweet;
If she the last wild aster meet,
    With fear its blue lips pale and quiver;
No gorgeous emblems of her might
She bears, yet in a single night
She thatches roofs with crystals white,
    And weaves ice-fringes on the river.

Her wild breath tosses to and fro
October's plumage, lying low,
Which, with her flurries of light snow
    She makes vain effort at concealing;
As with a veil of pleasantries
The wounded heart so often tries
To hide the scar that in it lies,
    When only time can bring it healing.

The perishing of fond desire,
Some mighty passion's burned out fire

Still smouldering on its funeral pyre,
    She seems forever pantomiming;
And yet, for all her sombre lays
And dull monotony of days,
The stricken heart must know always,
    Beyond, the Christmas bells are chiming.

A MEMORY.

I MARK it in the cooler rain,
    I read it on the curling fern:
The march of death steals on again,
    The gold and crimson hues return.

Once more the wild thorn's fruited top
    O'erhangs the cradle-knoll of ferns;
The beech-tree clasps again its crop,
    Again for it the squirrel yearns.

As lustily the cricket sings,
    As gorgeously the hill-tops glow,
Yet every hint of autumn brings
    Back one sad face of long ago.

And I can almost feel again '
  The pressure of one wasting hand;
And catch from lips, that knew no stain,
  Breathings, methinks, I understand.

Sometimes the whispers chide me so
  My quickened conscience pricks me sore;
Yet with new hope life is aglow,
  And peace my soul is flooding o'er.

THE WINTER WOODS.

How marvellous are draperies
They hang upon the dull gray skies!
How carelessly and with what grace
Their long brown arms reach into space!

The green moss shines amid the dark
Thick folds of their uneven bark;
And their boughs, nude and colorless,
The fingers of the wind caress.

A carpet underneath them lies
More fair than any tapestries

Which halls of Orient princes fill,
Or e'er was wrought by human skill.

Perchance some wizards in the night
Have hung them all with crystals bright,
Which flash on us from every limb,
Until our gazing eyes grow dim.

Again, like prophet's beards they glow,
O'erburdened with new-fallen snow,
Or seem, like spectres, weird and grand,
Inspiring awe on every hand.

Or each slim bough rare lace hangs on,
More wonderful than Honiton,
Which quivers in the icy air,
And gleams with splendor everywhere.

Now climbs the sun high o'er the woods,
And mellows with his wooing; floods
Of his warm breath over them sweep,
And all the tree-tops sob and weep.

And now the air grows chill and dense,
A cloud hangs over in suspense,

Then myriad petals downward fly
Out of the gardens of the sky.

Lo! every fern has fronds of white,
While every bush blooms in our sight;
And brake and briers bend to greet
White blossoms heaped up on their feet.

Amid rare works of art we stand,
Shaped by some mighty master's hand;
Unsightly stumps to statues grow,
Of Phidias or Angelo.

And groups of nymphs and fauns one sees,
Fair as those of Praxiteles;
Some temple must have stood near by,
For marble columns prostrate lie.

All things seem passionless and bare,
And yet divinely pure and fair,
And filled with silent melody,
And peace and sweet tranquillity.

THE UNATTAINED.

Joy is not in attaining,
 But comes in striving after;
 And days more filled with laughter
 Seem always somewhere just before
 Us; evermore
The best of all is that we fail in gaining.

The things we cannot climb to
 We hold the most inviting;
 Those freest, less requiting;
 The far-off bell another hears
 Beyond our ears,
Alas! we think there is a sweeter chime to.

That which we feast on cloys us;
 In what we taste some bliss is;
 But sweetest that one misses;
 Alas! for us! the heaven of each
 Is out of reach;
And with what most we long for fate decoys us.

SELF-MEASUREMENT.

Who feels the strength of purity
  Conceives not how sin can entice;
The last of all, therefore, is he
  To look to find in others vice.

Who entertains deceitfulness,
  Suspicion, too, invades his heart;
Since he thinks all must needs possess
  That of himself he knows a part.

OUR IDOL.

A tarnished reputation, it may be,
  The snows of time shall whiten out again;
A character once stained, eternity
  Itself, to make it spotless in, were vain.

With life men shield the reputation, though,
  And sport with character as if a toy;
Or, possibly, some thought on it bestow
  Lest it the reputation may destroy.

UNDER THE OAK.

WOOD-CAPPED hills above me rise;
  Near a river winds along;
Fairer than a poet's song
  Are the overarching skies.

Shadows come before the sun;
  Sombre grows my leafy bower;
Ah! the changes of an hour,
  Rain-drops falling one by one.

Quick a flash zigzags the sky;
  Back to earth the heavens roar;
Waiting till the storm is o'er,
  Underneath an oak I lie.

Bright o'er head again the sky;
  Changeful is the human heart;
Tears unasked like rain-drops start,
  And a laugh succeeds a sigh.

A WINTER SONG.

THE round high moon throws a misty light
      On forest and field below;
  With the cold of the night my fingers tingle,
And the frost is turning my chestnut white,
      As swiftly over the snow
      We merrily go,
  With bells that jingle, with bells that jingle.

The stream is frozen, the fences are white,
      And chill are the winds that blow;
  In many a song blithe voices mingle,
With many a laugh is startled the night,
      As flying over the snow
      We merrily go,
  With bells that jingle, with bells that jingle.

The moon rolls on, grows older the night,
      And the trees long shadows throw;
  Around the hill and down the dingle,—
Our hearts are warm though the drifts are white,
      As gliding over the snow
      We merrily go,
  With bells that jingle, with bells that jingle.

10

WHY DO WE LIVE? WHY DO WE DIE?

THE drop a passing cloud may spill,
The blighted leaf that falls before its time,
The crystal sun-kissed from its bed of rime,
    So narrow is the space we fill.

The yearning heart lifts up its cry,
We seek to know the way, and long for light
To see beyond the darkness of the night,
    But helplessly we strive, and die.

We climb up to some height and fall,
And grieve that we are hurled back to the ground;
What we have missed another soon has found,
    And God is ruling over all.

With tearful eyes to Death we give
Up one we think we cannot do without;
And all the world is wrapped in fear and doubt,
    God only knows why then we live.

And then we struggle hopelessly
When we feel that so much upon our lives
Depends, and death with life for mastery strives,
    God only knows why then we die.

We marvel at God's mystery,
And follow blindly where His hands may lead;
And this we only know, that hearts must bleed,
    And we must live, and we must die.

WATER-CRESSES.

ONE idling day,
Yet in life's May,
Some little seed of water-cress I flung away
Beside the cool, sweet waters of a haunted spring:
But, lo! I could not tell the harvest they would
    bring.

O'er land and sea,
As fate led me,
In waiting labor-fields I sought my destiny;

I sowed and tilled ; received men's curses and their
　　praise ;
Still toiled and strove through winter's cold and
　　summer's blaze.

Years afterward,
Again I heard
The song my old haunt's overflow of waters stirred ;
Far as the eye could see grew water-cresses rank ;
And, lo ! I traced them to the distant river's bank.

Life's harvesting,
What shall it bring ?
Oh, will the seed be like that scattered by the
　　spring ?
Its yield be manifold as water-cresses grow ?
But, lo ! I tremble sometimes lest it may be so.

REVELATION.

THE fleshly veil was lifted from my sight,
　　　　I dreamed ;
Two, whom I knew, revealed were in the light,
　　　　It seemed.

And I had fallen prostrate at the feet
  Of one,—the idol of my heart was she;
But one in fellowship I did not greet,
  So wide the gulf between, apparently.

But disentranced, I loathe and scorn the thing
  I loved, so full of cruel black deceit;
And that pure soul I spurned, lo! worshipping,
  I kiss the ground whereon have pressed her feet.

LOVE MARKS THE SEASON.

WHEN desolation holds its sway,
  And hearts are cold and love is dead,
    And friendship's warmth is waning,
  Though fragrant bloom the locusts shed,
For all the lark's sweet carols say,
    The winter months are reigning.

When hope is brave, and love is king,
  And lives are linked with endless vows,
    And hearts cease from repining,
  Though fierce winds scar the naked boughs,
For all the lake's cold covering,
    The summer days are shining.

OUR KING.

Four fingers, mellow as a plum,
　　Fit but to be caressed and kissed,
With just a wee bit of a thumb
　　Rolled up into a dainty fist.

On either foot five tiny toes,
　　All coiled up in a little heap,
And every toe pink as a rose,
　　The tally of a dimple deep.

Like sunbeams curled up on the head
　　Lie amber tufts of silken hair;
For cheeks two peaches round and red,
　　And dimples, dimples everywhere.

Bits of the blue of heaven the eyes,
　　Tip of a lily's bud the nose;
And when he laughs and when he sighs,
　　Two pink-lined pearls unclasp and close.

He cannot work, he cannot think,
  Yet he is wise and cunning too;
And he can smile, and he can wink
  More easily than graybeards do.

He cannot talk, he cannot sing,
  And hardly climbs along the floor;
But of an empire he is king,
  And never king like him before.

HOW KIND IS DEATH!

As all now see the wan, sweet face
  Of her who lies there peacefully,
Remembrance of her bloom and grace,
  Through all the years to come will be.

Yet I know that before their eyes
  I must grow old with every breath;
And so my heart in anguish cries,
  How cruel life; how kind is death!

KING SHAM.

SINCE the fiat supreme was spoken,
And the reign of chaos broken,
  Many rulers great and small
    Have lived their day,
    And held their sway
  Upon this terrestrial ball;
  Yet the mightiest monarch of all
    Is the great King Sham.

Ere old Rome had one to defend her,
Ere the dawn of Grecian splendor,
  Or the march of Xenophon;
    Ere the Iliad was sung,
    Or the gardens hung
  Of the gorgeous Babylon:
  Who can tell when the reign was begun
    Of the great King Sham?

Though the empires of ancient story,
Of whose warrior kings the glory
  And valor are told in song,

Fell into decay,
And vanished away,
Through weakness and vice and wrong,
Yet the weakness of men makes strong
The great King Sham.

To him we are vassals ever,—
And another such tyrant never
Has ruled on the earth anywhere;
For, whom we shall meet,
And when we shall eat,
What the tint shall be of our hair,
And the heel of the shoe we wear,
Decrees King Sham.

His subjects he takes from all stations
In life; for in all occupations
Men are eager to do his will;
His prey are the whole;
He has control
Of traffic, of counter, and till,
And grinds at every man's mill,
The great King Sham.

He assumes all manner of graces,
Though false at all times and places,
  And always a despot still;
    The stripes of our socks,
    The cut of our frocks,
  Or whatever garments we fill,
  All are work—and so is the bill—
    Of the great King Sham.

He allures and dazzles and flatters
With the gilded baubles he scatters,
  Till the vision blinds our eyes;
    His mockeries to vice
    And folly entice,
  And we break the holiest ties
  And our very souls sacrifice
    To the great King Sham.

What tax he levies we bear it,
Though we live in a cellar or garret,
  And cash and the coal-bin are low;
    Though we bite of a crust,
    Yet serve him we must,
  For out of his kingdom we go,
  If ever we dare to say no
    To the great King Sham.

He fashions from pulpit to steeple
The place where his worshipping people
  Are wont to gather to pray;
    And living or dead,
    If we die or are wed,
  The proper amount of display
  Becoming, is gauged alway
    By the great King Sham.

Seek the law, whether saint or sinner
You are proven to be, ever thinner
  And thinner your pocket-book grows;
    One pleads your case,
    One paints your disgrace,
  The jurors the verdict disclose;
  How to beat him who wins it, knows
    The great King Sham.

The doctor one calls; first he scares him,
Then, maybe, a little repairs him,
  And a marvellous cure is done
    With his mighty skill,
    Or magical pill;
  So from everything under the sun,
  Tribute and glory are won
    For the great King Sham.

You buy wheat,—it is nothing but paper;
Your profit is nothing but vapor,
  Though you painfully realize
    It if luck goes wrong;
    Then you sing a new song,
  And quickly open your eyes,
  Alas! to the cunning that lies
    In the great King Sham.

Not till truth than falsehood is dearer,
And our soul-lit vision is clearer,
  Will the strength of this monarch wane;
    But who can foretell
    When the magical spell
  Of his power will be rent in twain,
  Or the end of the farcical reign
    Of the great King Sham?

If only true gold were gleaming
And yellow, if always the seeming
  Were real and true, and within
    Was always the grace
    That we read on the face,
  And the heart had no hidden sin,
  The ruin would surely begin
    Of the great King Sham.

Sometimes, in the midst of our sorrow,
Is cheer in the thought of a morrow,
　When that sorrow will be no more;
　　When toil is done,
　　And our crowns are won,
　And we cross to the other shore
　At last, the sway will be o'er
　　Of the great King Sham.

WARNING.

I saw a red, red bud unfolding
　Its beauty to the quickening air;
I saw two red lips that were burning
　With prisoned kisses,—hearts, beware!

The rose's red petals yet shall shatter
　The pitiless blast of the rain;
Red lips, what heart for you shall quiver
　And break, pierced through with bitterest pain?

MY NEIGHBOR.

My neighbor's garden blossoms fair
  With rose and pink and daffodil;
  In vain my efforts are to till,
And all my fields are bleak and bare.

My neighbor's mill brings him in toll
  From all there be who come thereto;
  My own brown hands have work to do
The while love's thrill goes through my soul.

My neighbor has some store of gold,
  And I have memories to keep;
  My toil each day each night brings sleep,
And in some hearts a place I hold.

My neighbor's vineyard, fair to see,
  Has purple grapes a clustering;
  Each morn a bluebird comes to sing
A little song just made for me.

My neighbor has much to him given,
 A heritage of wealth and lands;
 My heritage is just two hands,
And work gives law, but love makes heaven.

Yet, while love's strength uplifts my hands,
 My heart need not go hungering,
 My heart need not be envying
My neighbor's riches or his lands.

THE SPIRIT OF THE BELL.

I STOOD far underneath a mighty dome;
 The air grew tremulous with giant throes
Of its far-reaching bell; "Why have you come?
 What is your mission here to-day?"
 As each one through the open portals goes,
 The bell's loud spirit seemed to say.

Upon the brow of each unconsciously
 Was borne some characters I could not read,
It seemed, until an angel read for me;

So each man's heart to me was shown;
No matter what his race, or cloth, or creed,
His secret thoughts to me were known.

Men came with saintly mien and lordly sway,
Great in their own conceit, and swelled with pride,
As if they were made of some better clay,
Who mingled with this motley throng,
And grandly swung within the portals wide,
Whose hearts, I saw, were black with wrong.

Some came with evil purposes intent,
With features that had something yet of grace,
Whose hearts were all with passion soiled and rent;
And there were those who pressed within
Who sought through voice of men to gain high
place,
And hither came to favor win.

And I saw enter there a stately dame
In robe that fashion her approval gave;
She bore an ancient and respected name,
Her hands in jewelled splendor shone.
Yet in the toils of sin she writhed, a slave,
Her heart to honor dead as stone.

And some whose souls were stained with crime, I
      saw,
  Whom fear had led into this holy place,
And not remorse; whom vengeance of the law
    Awaited, swift and sure, if known,
  Who yet with characters veneered with grace
    In stolen garb of Christians shone.

But there were many, with such modest ways,
  On whom at first my eyes did scarcely rest,
Who seemed unconscious of the public's gaze,
    Or of themselves, who meekly went
  Within, and in humility confessed
    That in Christ's love they were content;

That to the angel that beside me stood
  I turned and prayed that he would blind my eyes
Again, that I might only know the good,
    And that I nevermore might see
  The wickedness in human hearts that lies,
    But think all as they seem to be.

The spirit of the bell rang out once more,
  And, as if in its last expiring throe,
More thrilling seemed than it had been before:

11*

"To search thy neighbor's heart is vain
To find wrong in thine own, O Mortal, know!"
And I was pierced with mighty pain.

ALL IN ALL.

WHEN I shall look into your face
   And find not there the boon I crave,
And in your glance no longer trace
   The outlines of the love you gave
And pledged me with your sacred vow,
   Though on my face warm is your breath,
And hot blood flushes yet your brow,
   Oh, then, to me, it will be death.

But while I know that, all in all,
   I am to you and you to me,
That, weal or woe, whate'er befall,
   Our love cannot divided be,
Your dimming eyes in death may close,
   Your throbbing pulse may cease its strife,
By magic that love only knows,
   To me, e'en then there will be life.

LOVE'S MESSENGER.

OFF of the waste of emerald lea
  Under my feet,
A wild red rose I pluck for thee,
  My sweet!

If touched once by thy finger-tips,
Or breathed upon by thy fair lips,
And heat or cold, by breath that blows,
Or glance out of thine eye it knows,
  And thou dost send it back to me,
   Though all its petals lose their red,
  And it shall wither in my grasp,
   And seem to die,
  The rose will not to me be dead,
Which once the pressure of thy clasp
   Has known; yet I
  In each brown leaf a rose shall see,
And breathings of its perfume rare
Something of thee to me shall bear.

But if thou crush it with thy feet,
　Oh, would that I, then, it might be,
To know if any agony
　In death by thee can be, my sweet!

THE DIFFERENCE.

WHEN she was five, and I was ten,
　Implicitly she did obey me;
For slightest favors shown her then,
　With rapturous kisses she did pay me.

I cared but little for her then,
　But little, too, I cared to please her;
And I was most delighted when
　I could find some new way to tease her.

Now she is seventeen, and I,
　A youth of twenty-two, would woo her;
But I quail now before her eye,
　And tremble when I come near to her.

My lips refuse to make appeal
　To this, the fairest of all misses;
Though I would be her slave, to feel
　The rapture of one of her kisses.

A VALENTINE.

A VAST and dreary waste of drifted snow
  Extended far as human eye can see;
A piercing air, and yon and hither blow
  The fleecy flakes as changeful winds decree,—
  Sure harbingers of deeper drifts to be;
The clouds hang low, and all the gloomy day
The sun, obscure, sends out no kindling ray;
  Snow crowns the roof, icicles fringe the eaves;
  On window-panes the frost his lace-work weaves;
The swaying tree-tops sing a mournful lay;
  The yeoman grieves o'er cold and care and kine,
The traveller mourns o'er drifts that clog his way;
  And yet, what warmth, what cheer, oh, heart of
    mine!
  Can cold chill love, my sweet, my valentine?

THISTLE-DOWN.

Go, thistle-down, that idly drifts the drowsy air,
  I speed thee with my breath!
Go, softly press her brow than lily is more fair,
The breathings of my burning passion to her bear;

If any glance up from her eye divine,
 Aught in it hath
Betokens peace unto the heart of mine,
Come, whisper it to me, O thistle-down.

Come, thistle-down, adrift upon the lazy air,
 Stirred by her gentle breath:
Too long you linger in caresses of her hair,
The breathing of her stainless lips unto me bear;
 If voice or flaming cheeks give any sign
  That gladdeneth,
 Or bringeth peace unto the heart of mine,
Come, whisper it to me, O thistle-down.

COLUMBINE.

Nodding as her fleet
Footsteps pass, the clover-blossoms greet her,
 Columbine,
 Darling mine;
 Sipping ruby wine,
In their passion's heat,
From her lips so sweet,

Zephyr-lovers idly roaming meet her,
　　Bend down to her feet,
Kiss and make the clover-blossoms sweeter.

　　With a lily's grace
Charmed, a sunbeam lover would secure her;
　　　Columbine,
　　　Darling mine,
　　Then his arms entwine:
　　Kisses touch her face;
　　Warmed in the embrace,
Back then goes the cunning lover, surer,
　　To the trysting place,
Kisses, wins, and makes the lily purer.

EGLANTINE.

MANY gems of the earth are fair;
　　But a queen divine
　　Is my Eglantine,—
A jewel never so rare.

Was ever so charming a lass?
　　Clover-blossoms sweet
　　Salute her feet
As her magic footsteps pass.

She plucks at her own sweet will
　　The daintiest flowers
　　Of the woodland bowers,
Which for her rich fragrance distil.

Bright buttercups bend with grace
　　As she wanders nigh,
　　And the wind, stealing by,
Kisses perfume sweet from her face.

To innocent beauty weds,
　　Since her lips fade the rose;
　　And, when near them she goes,
The violets bend their heads.

Fresh plucked from the white fields nigh,
　　The many-rayed wreath
　　Of the daisy's her teeth,
And a sapphire gem is each eye.

Cupid's arrow, golden-tipped,
    Is each word she speaks;
    And the pearl of her cheeks
In the flush of the morning is dipped.

In her power and modesty meet;
    In the presence serene
    Of this magical queen
The forces of evil retreat.

Her touch is of heaven a gleam;
    As the stars as fair,
    She reigns everywhere,
And her heart is love supreme.

A vision or real? Hast thou place,
    O spirit divine,
    Fairest Eglantine?
Or a poet's dream is thy grace?

WHITE AND BLUE.

She was in the garden,
  In a gown of white and blue
That was just bewitching:
  Noiselessly I nearer drew,
Not a word was spoken,
  As an arm around I threw,
Holding fast a pretty
  Little waist of white and blue.

It was in the twilight,
  In the shadow of the pine,
That I came upon her,
  And so near—her face and mine—
Each one touched a wing of
  Something that between them flew;
And I thought so pretty
  Was her gown of white and blue.

THROUGH THE YEAR.

In spring, on every lea,
  From every chaste, coy violet,
There seems to flash on me
  The very eye of Margaret.

The songs of summer days,
  Ah me! can I their thrill forget,
When in the sweetest lays
  I hear the voice of Margaret?

In autumn, when each tree
  Some wizard has with rubies set;
Ah! then I only see
  The flushing cheeks of Margaret.

In winter, when soft flakes
  Out of the dreary skies are let,
One thought in me awakes,—
  So white the soul of Margaret.

GOLD-THREAD.

WHILE yet the banks are dank and cold
   And hardly know the warmth of sun,
Whose touch the red buds makes unfold
   And life-blood of the birches run,
A tiny stem shoots up its head,
   And spreads out its white canopy
Above the litter of the dead
   Leaves that around it lie.

Brave as the winds that snap and break
   The twigs of dead boughs o'er its head,
And spotless as the purest flake
   The winter tossed upon its bed;
One marvels at the sweet, pale lips,
   And at the tale by them is told:
Hid in the turf from which it slips
   Are many threads of gold.

Sweet herald of the fuller bloom,
   It turns its face up to the sky,
And trembles not at its near doom;
   So frail a blossom needs must die,

And swift the march of its decay;
  Yet glowing shields of dusky green
Shall haunt and guard, for many a day,
  The place it once has been.

Through all these wintry years of ours,
  Set here and there are sunny days
With bloom and fragrance of white flowers,
  That beautify our roughest ways;
And though all bleak and bare and cold
  A life seems, sometimes, outwardly,
We know bright gleaming threads of gold
  Within it somewhere lie.

––––––––––

THE WOOING OF THE ROSE.

On a rose-bush lazily
  Climbing the garden wall,
  The fairest rose of all
Was wooed by a butterfly.

A graceful dandy was he,
  With dazzling, delicate wings
  All covered with spangles and rings,—
"But I love you not," said she.

And so, without more ado,
  To the cloud-land flew the gay,
  Faint-hearted lover away;
And the next that came to woo

Was a youth, as bold as needs be,
  With a brownish, tidy suit,
  And a sword, and mighty and cute,
And a marvel of industry.

He hummed her many an air,
  And sang of the marvellous walls
  In his own ancestral halls,
And the treasures gathered there.

Of her riches she gave him part,
  And loaded him down with gold
  All his tiny sacks would hold,
But he could not win her heart.

Then a dew-drop, seeing the fire
  Of her gown as it flamed its light
  On the gathering gloom of night,
Besought her with mad desire.

Again and again her red,
  Sweet lips were bathed in his wine;
  "Evermore I will be thine,"
He sang, as he rolled in her bed.

But the night was gone, and the dew,
  And a silver sunbeam came,
  And the heart of the rose was aflame;
Still redder her petals grew,

And fairer than ever before;
  But, alas! for the fickle thing
  She fell to withering,
And his kisses revived her no more.

Then the wind came dancing along
  With bewitching sorceries
  And musical cadences,
And whispered to her a sweet song.

She was shaken as never before
When he made his caressing plea;
"Only go with me," said he,
"And we'll roam the wide world o'er."

But he tore her petals apart,
And scattered them one by one,
And left her dishonored, alone,
To die of a broken heart.

MY HOLLYHOCKS.

My hollyhocks the amorous breeze
Let sip out of their chalices
The aromatic wines they hold;
While his long arms their waists enfold,
And they reel just as he decrees.

From far across the shining leas
Fly greedy, brown-winged honey bees,
To rifle of their mellow gold
My hollyhocks.

These lovers dally as they please,
And fondle their sweet mistresses;
  To pluck their hearts the bees are bold;
  The wind is wroth, grows rough and cold,
And, bearing off his rivals, frees
    My hollyhocks.

THE DAISY.

A THOUSAND perfect gems, wrought out of earth
    and mist and light,
  Into one amber disk are locked;
Rare jewels circle it around with rays of spotless
    white;
  By all the meadow breezes rocked,
    Upon its willow wand it swings,
    This marvel that the summer brings,
      The daisy.

A myriad of weaknesses by burning lips confess,
  And passion's pain and passion's strife
Have entered in my soul, disfiguring its loveliness;
  But He can bless a sin-stained life,

And bleach its darkness into light,
Whose hands have made so clean and white
The daisy.

ANEMONE.

UPON an edge
Of a rock, underneath a tree
Overhanging a ledge
I found an anemone.

In so rough a place
How grew ye, fragile gem,
So worthy to grace
A queen's own diadem?

Oh, tell me, brave
One, nursed in a barren home,
The secret you have,—
Through sorrows do graces come?

Is this what you say,—
No heart is so bleak and bare
But germs we may
Find of love and beauty there?

Must we blossoms gain
Of resignation sweet
On the heights of pain,
Which we scale with wounded feet?

Can only the stone
That bruises, the plant give a root,
From which full-blown
White flowers of forgiveness shoot?

LAPPA.

EACH flower has its place,
Some one gives it embrace,
Some poet sings its grace,
But outcasts are thy race.

It seems to be thy fate
To seek haunts desolate,
And grow and propagate
Without the garden gate.

But thou inspirest me,
Lappa, to sing to thee,
In that so patiently
Thou bearest ills that be.

I praise thee for thy pluck:
With spade or mattock struck,
However hard thy luck,
Thy head is upward stuck.

Men scoff at thee and swear,
Thy cumbrous leaves they tear,
Thy trunks close down they pare,
But thou dost live and bear.

Thy perfume men despise,
Thy bloom they ostracize;
Yet in thy purple lies
Some beauty to my eyes.

Affectionately cling
The bracts encompassing
Thy flowers, though withering
Or dead, to everything.

And though men curse, they bless
Thee sometimes in distress;
The virtue they confess
E'en of thy bitterness.

And God made thee for good,
To live with fortitude
Thy life of hardihood;
Could I shield thee, I would;

For wrongs that give thee smart
Wake pity in my heart;
Keep, though, from me apart,—
I like thee—where thou art.

HEART'S-EASE.

ONCE, when my love was grieving,
  A tear fell from her eye;
Out of the earth receiving
  It, grew a pansy by and by.

But in the face upturning
  Of that low, tear-born flower
The same dark eye was burning,
  Whose glances thrilled me with their power.

SWEET-CLOVER.

WHY didst thou tremble, sweet-clover,
  When that brown-winged rover went by,
And nearer and nearer did hover,
  And then straight down to thee fly?

Did thy sweetheart call thee his deary?
  Or what did he say to thee?
Do ever thy ears grow weary
  Of his strange, wild minstrelsy?

Thy lovers are robbers, sweet-clover;
  Thy fragrance afar they scent;
They plunder thee over and over,
  And will till thy sweetness is spent.

When the flush of thy bloom shall leave thee,
  And the days of thy beauty are o'er,
Sweet-clover, then will it grieve thee
  If thy wooers come back nevermore?

AS GOD WILLS.

THE workings of Thy hand
  Mysterious are, Almighty God!
We cannot understand
  Inflictions of Thy chastening rod.

Are we so sorely tried
  To teach humility below?
Are pleasures here denied
  The better heavenly joys to know?

Why suffering and woe,
  If love and mercy reign above?
Doubt readily whispers low,
  "God rules not with the hand of love."

The voice of Wisdom cries
  Aloud, "All worketh well for good;
But blessings in disguise,
  Afflictions rightly understood."

Does not the blackest night
  Oft come before a day most fair?
The crashing thunder's might
  Foretell a softer, purer air?

They stand the battle storm
  Who would the victor's laurels wear;
What matter if some form
  Of burden every day we bear?

Oh, drain without complaint
   The bitter cup unto thee borne;
Let not thy spirit faint,
   There yet shall come a brighter morn.

God rules with loving hand;
   Oh, question not His love, although
We cannot understand
   Always why He chastises so.

O Faith! point onward still;
   O God! grant strength to stand each test;
We bow unto Thy will,
   Oh, lead us whither seemeth best.

INVOCATION.

THE way which Thou hast marked for me to go,
   Dear Lord, oh, let that way be mine!
The thing which Thou hast planned for me to know,
   That knowledge, Lord, let me divine;

The one thing Thou hast now for me to do,
　Grant me the strength to do to-day;
And whatsoe'er Thou leadest me unto,
　Help me that to accept alway.

Each passing hour vouchsafed to me, dear Lord,
　In this great gift of life I take
From Thee; oh, let each thought, and deed, and
　　word,
　Help me the most of it to make;
So shall I climb up to my destiny;
　And, though the path be hard and steep,
I know that my weak hands will strengthened be
　Always with Thy love, strong and deep.

OH, PRAISE HIS HOLY NAME!

GOD's sky is overhead,
　God's fields beneath our feet;
　　Above, below,
　　All creatures know
His love; the poppy's red,
　The pansy's hue, the sweet

Of rose
God's love bestows,—
Oh, praise his holy name!

God's sun lights up the day,
  God's stars illume the night;
    Behold his love!
    Below, above,
O'er all things it has sway;
  The glow-worm's tiny light
    Is his,
    The lightning is,—
Oh, praise His holy name!

God's rain falls on the earth,
  God's rainbow spans the skies;
    His love, behold,
    How manifold!
Riches of untold worth
  Pour from His treasuries;
    His hand
    Makes glad the land,—
Oh, praise His holy name!

God's waters fill the seas,
  And all in them are His;
    No living thing
    But owns Him king,
  And bows to His decrees;
    For all His mercy is;
      No cry
      He passes by,—
Oh, praise His holy name!

EASTER LILIES.

A SCENT of lilies in the air,—
A hint of gladness everywhere,—
  Broken the seal to-day,
  The stone is rolled away.

With fragrance earth so flooding o'er:
So fair were lilies e'er before?
  All doubt is swept away,
  Is what the lilies say.

Oh, lilies pure, oh, lilies white,
Ye tokens of the holy light,
    Enfolding us alway,
    And turning night to day!

Hail sacred morning, come again
With your glad message unto men!
    The Christ arose to-day,
    Is what your lilies say.

With pallid lips, with sorrow dumb,
No more they tremble at the tomb
    Where He was laid away,—
    The Saviour rose to-day.

Bring lilies, then, white lilies bring,—
His love will crown our offering;
    And men shall bless for aye
    The Lord who rose to-day.

AN EASTER GREETING.

Day of days to mortal men,
Light of all the centuries,
Hope of ages yet unborn,
Harbinger of joys supernal,
Hail, oh, sacred morn!
Garland it with lilies white,
Pure as its unfading light;
Through the darkness of death's night
Glory shines of morn eternal.
All the universe rejoices,
And with myriad gentle voices,
Slumbering nature, waking, cries:
"He is risen, nothing dies;"
All her icy clasps unclose,
And again to life are stirred
Germs, that, underneath the snows,
In a wintry trance have lain;
Though ye wither, though ye rot,
Death and cold ye crush in vain,
Since the bloom returns again.

Every tender blade that springs
From the mould of meadows bleak,
Heralding the harvesting;
Every soft, sweet note of bird
As it mates and nests and sings,—
E'en the lazy worm that lies
In the sunbeam, fattening
For the hungry robin's beak,—
Each its wealth of promise brings,
All of Him arisen speak;
Though the struggle and the cry,
Though the death-wound and the smart,
Evermore the crown is nigh;
Jesus lives, and death is not;
It is written everywhere,—
In the winds, more softly blowing,
In the sun, more brightly glowing,
In the streams, more freely flowing,
In the red buds, redder growing,
In the fields, and in the skies,
In the lilies,—in all things;
In the yearnings of the heart,
In each hope and in each prayer.

RECEIVE ME.

To no one have I done a wrong,—
  Lord, who of us can say it?
  Thy anger, wilt Thou stay it?
Receive me! this my song
Is all day long.

And I have not corrupted one,—
  Oh, could we only know it!
  Lord, may Thy record show it;
Receive me, Father, Son,
When toil is done.

And I have taken only mine,—
  There is not one that liveth
  Hath aught save what God giveth;
Receive me into Thine
Own, Lord divine!

CHANCE.

WHERE fallow fields are fierce and desolate,
  Beside which winds a roadway thinly grown
  With sickly plants, whose germs the winds have
    blown
From far, and wantonly left to their fate;
Where fearless woos the bird his timid mate
  In tangled copse to sunlight scarcely known,
  Or clumps of ferns along the marshes strown;
Where all things seem in quite abandoned state,
  Hemmed in with luxury of wilderness,
    I came upon a sweet, fair clover-bed.
Ah me! our ways from birth until we die
  Lie over marsh and moor, or more or less,
    And thither we are often blindly led
To blessings where we little think they lie.

TEST.

IF to some goal on which is set the heart
   We tend, and nearness makes desire expand;
   If, as we almost reach it with the hand,
Most unexpectedly some foe upstart,
And thrust between, keep us and it apart,
   Upsetting all our daring hope has planned,—
   To bear and break not, then, but firmly stand,
Unswayed from right by hate or passion's art;
   To bow submissively to fate adverse,
And cherish in our inmost heart for him
   Who does this wrong no bitterness; to curse
Him not, but pray his cup up to the brim
   With joy be filled,—and leave to God the rest,—
   Divinest love, this is thy crowning test.

SUBMISSION.

THINK you that all is lost because your plans,
  Born of conceit, fail of their fulfilment?
  If in wild aim your bullet's force is spent?
The kindest breeze of heaven, it may be, fans
The flame that fires the bridge that the chasm spans,
  Beyond which lies the goal on which are bent
  Your longing eyes.   Oh, mortal, be content
To follow,—let the lead be God's, not man's;

Life is not judged by one unfruitful hour;
  Wait to the end.   God's mills grind slow indeed;
    Yet giant oaks spring from bitter acorns;
  Some sad experience may be the seed
From which developed is the perfect flower,
    Which most the life enriches and adorns.

TRUST.

This very moment there may lie around
  Us very near some overwhelming proof
  Of want but half concealed by lowly roof,
Which stands away but by a space from ground
Where ostentatious luxuries abound;
  But by a space, perchance, she stands aloof,
  With woven robes of golden warp and woof,
From her with needful clothing poorly gowned.

Why one must strive for sustenance in vain,
  And boundless riches fill the greedy hand
Another holds till surfeit is a pain,
  O God, not now we seek to understand;
That must be best Thy righteous hands let fall,
And somewhere compensation waits for all.

UNSATISFIED.

How many of my days are numbered! and
  How little of that which in flush of youth
  I thought to do has yet been done! forsooth,
Along the years my narrow life has spanned
Are legions of wrecked hopes,—a spectral band;
  Alas! how well I know their forms uncouth,—
  Each idol shattered and each bitter truth!
Who else each failure's woe can understand?

When of despair, sometimes the burden seems
  More than the fainting spirit can endure;
And heart, grown stubborn and suspicious, deems
  The sources of all longed-for things impure,
Does only darkness hang upon the days
Because the eyes are blind to all God's ways?

14*

INDECISION.

DAY after day unstaying years go by,
  And we grope our uncertain, halting way
  Along the base of heights we should essay
To climb, upon whose summits lifted high
The jewelled coronets of honor lie.
  One sees with vision clear as sunlight's ray
  His chance or calling, and with no delay
He pushes on until the goal is nigh,
  And men at his success are stricken dumb,
And all the world his daring genius hails.
  Oh, ye alert, when fateful moments come,
A tear for them whom fortune always fails!
  Who, seeing not the end, fear to begin,
  And pass by opportunities to win.

CONSCIENTIOUSNESS.

WHO never turn from beaten paths away,
   And, without questioning, life's goal pursue,
   Accepting for the best each common view,
Find sympathy, approval, strength, and stay
In sweet companionship from day to day;
   While often he, to his convictions true,
   Who dares to venture in some pathway new,
Traditions old refusing longer sway,
   Finds fierce antagonisms, distrust, and hate;
Yet following where his conscious duties lead;
He is a man and hero true, indeed,
   Who heeds not reputation, peace, or fate,
Or public praise, dear unto mortal ears,
Unless beyond the voice of God he hears.

MANHOOD.

MEN sing his praise who scales some mountain
    height
  Which never yet has trodden mortal's feet;
  Whom genius crowns all men with honor greet;
And men respect him who upholds with might,
At whate'er cost, whate'er he thinks is right;
  Whose sword wins fame, to him are honors meet;
  But whom we love most, though, his life is sweet
And pure; and hopefully, from morn till night,
He strives day after day, year after year,
  With willing hands and tireless feet, in ways
His lines are cast; he holds truth more than greed,
And all high place at cost of honor dear;
  And rather than his sacred trust betrays,
He calmly faces death, if there be need.

MORE LIGHT.

THE rocks entombed in earth impatient lie,
  And into light are whirled through openings wide
  Of mountains which their giant throes divide;
The little seeds, though buried, do not die,
But blade and leaf and tree leap towards the sky;
  "More light!" cried Goethe, with his dying
      breath;
  More light! the song of birth, the throe of
      death!
More light! of nature all the yearning cry
  Since God creation's morn the dawn proclaimed;
Men probe the earth: her treasures gives the sea;
  The darkness yields unto the lightning tamed,
Nor yet does science cease her prophecy;
  Still man, for light, shall grope through night
      and sin,
  Until God's presence he shall enter in.

A SUMMER DAY.

ACROSS the intervening valley wide
  The emerald hill-tops kiss the sapphire sky;
  In swaying hammock lazily I lie
And trace the line where green and blue divide,
Or watch the banks of foamy clouds that ride
  Above me as I listen dreamily
  To melodies among the boughs near by,
Loud trilled from throats which yellow-green
     leaves hide.
The cooling zephyrs breathe upon my face,
  And every breath has balm of many flowers.
    Oh, golden day of dear midsummer time,
Spellbound in thy voluptuous embrace,
  I yield up grudgingly the passing hours,
  And mourn thy fading hue the while I rhyme.

A MARCH DAY.

DUMB in their nests the sparrows cheerless lie;
  The clouds low down are draped with folds of
      black,
  Which almost touch the boughs of tamarack,
Through which the fierce wind's breath sweeps
      mournfully;
Across the narrow, lifeless street, near by,
  An unclean snow-drift lingers; farther back
  I trace the surging river's yellow track,
Between its tawny willow guards, whose high
    Heads quiver in the melancholy gloom,
Pervading all the earth and air and sky;
  When, lo! through riven clouds the sunlight
      breaks;
    Supernal glories earth and sky illume;
And all my heart to new-born raptures wakes,
And all my thoughts of Him I magnify.

AT THE BRIDGE.

ENRAPTURED with the glowing wood-crowned hills,
  At quiet sunset hour alone I stand
  Above this stream with iron sinews spanned,
And all my being with the beauty thrills,
And all my spirit with the glory fills;
  Out from the riven cloud a golden band
  Lights up the barren drifts of yellow sand;
The breathless hush my throbbing pulses stills.

While round the bar with graceful sweep and bend,
Scioto's waters with Ohio's blend,—
  So when the victories of life are won,
    May its sunset with holy light draw nigh;
  So merge time and eternity in one,
    As river glides to river peacefully.

THE WIND.

Is it the ghosts of the midsummer bees
   That sting and haunt me this November day?
   Comes from the south a breeze chilled on its way
In sipping ices on the frosted leas?
Or sweeps some wild blast from the northern seas?
   It tosses up and scourges in its play
The brown discarded jewels of the trees,
   And in its mockery it seems to say,—
"In splendor you have flaunted one brief hour
   Your finery; behold your glory now!
      I wear no crimson gowns, yet roam the sky;
   I fan the vales and kiss the mountain's brow,
      And lapse of time and bounds of space defy;
And you,—lo, I can crush you with my power."

15

PROMISE.

CHILL is the south wind's breath, the clouds hang
    low ;
Around me lie great·drifts of melting snow ;
A smithy's anvil near is silent, forge
    Fireless,—it is the holy Sabbath day ;
    A bridge of stone along the travelled way
Extends, and underneath leaps down the gorge
    A swollen stream, with foam and splash and
      spray ;
On distant hill-tops rests the fog ; below,
O'er flat submerged, the shimmering waters flow ;
    A gloomy morn, suggesting all sad things,
    Yet all the misty air with music rings ;
For, on the topmost bough of maple near
And bare and lone, with breast aflame, loud, clear,
    A prophet of the summer sweetly sings.

SPITZKOP.

(February 27, 1881.)

FEAR not, thou heaven-inspired, heroic band,
  Whose valor's deeds fill freemen's hearts to-day;
  Your cause is just; what despot's power can stay,
When struggling freedom lifts her holy hand
To strike the foe that grasps her fatherland?
  Proud leader of the nations, turn away!
  A people just endure, the wrong decay;
Ancestral kingdom, name historic, grand,
  Is this thy chivalry, that England's might
  Shall crush the weak and trample on the right?
The gods make mad and then destroy,—beware!
  They lose who 'gainst the God of battles fight;
Guard well thy ancient name and fame! They
    dare
In righteous cause who heroes' laurels wear.

OUR UNWELCOME FRIEND.

THERE is a sentinel with watchful eyes,
  Alert day after day, year after year,
  Who signals us when there is danger near;
Who stays our sports, our best-laid plans defies;
If we transgress too far in anywise,
  Quite apt he is unbidden to appear;
  Although his voice we hardly ever hear,
Unless we cross the line where safety lies.
  There is no truer friend of man; and yet
We do not love him,—oh, base ingratitude!
  For mortals who his warning cries forget
Curse him whose only mission is their good.
  Who is this slave who serves and seeks no gain,
  This angel unawares? Men call him—Pain.

LUNA AD TELLUREM.

THROUGH regions boundless, far, unquestioning,
  While myriad cycles roll, I go with thee,
  A helpless slave, on to my destiny;
What light illumines me to thee I fling;
To thy weird path through heat and cold I cling,
  And hang my crescent o'er thy land and sea;
  Methinks, if thou dost sometimes tire of me,
Thou canst not then escape my following.
What mystic force my fate links to thine, Earth?
  For I have felt the pressure of thy clasp
Since roving planets had from chaos birth;
  Above, beneath, forever in thy grasp,
Thy torch, thy toy, I marvel at thy might,
Yet serve thee, queen, a loyal satellite.

15*

BETRAYAL.

WE sigh to see the things we long for go,
　　When we know that to strive for them is vain,
　　To feel they never will be near again;
To see the face we love still whiter grow,
As death steals on to strike the fatal blow.
　　Oft conscious worth must writhe in galling
　　　　chain,
　　And ecstasy of love be pierced with pain,
For every heart its bitterness must know.

All mourn some aspiration unfulfilled,
　　And taste the anguish of some fond hopes dead,
　　　Or grieve for some lost friend whom they have
　　　　prized;
　　But death's own darkness pales in that night's
　　　　dread
Awakening, which comes ere throbs are stilled
　　Of heart by its betrayal paralyzed.

THE UNEXPECTED.

THE things with great anxiety one strives
   For do not satisfy him in the end:
   But seldom peace fulfilment does attend;
The deepest woe or joy supremest thrives
Most on the unexpected in our lives;
   As o'er the barren waste our way we tend,
   The lone flower that we pluck seems like a friend
Who in some dire extremity arrives;
Its perfume gladdens us as does the sight
   Of a familiar face we rest the eyes
      Upon amid the surging crowd of some
Strange thoroughfare. When Death with sudden
      might
   Strikes one we love, our loss he magnifies
    More than if heralded his footsteps come.

AT THE LAKE.

I SIT and dream beside the placid meer;
　Through amber haze the sunlight warms the wold;
　On crimson tapestries and beds of gold,
Across the bay, the skies to rest appear;
And in the mirror at my feet, so near,
　Rubies in gorgeous clusters I behold,
　And amethysts and sapphires manifold.
Oft in the autumn of a by-gone year,
　When these old trees were painted every hue,
Another came and rested with me here,
　Under their boughs, beside these waters blue,
For evermore to memory so dear;
　One now beneath the withered grasses lies,
　While overhead still glow the mocking skies.

NOT YET.

So much to say, so many songs to sing,
  So many things I cannot now forget,
  So much to do that I cannot leave yet.
O Death, a little longer let me cling
To these, if it must be, with suffering;
  I did not think that I must pay the debt
  To thee, and leave all else with such regret,
While yet I longed so much for everything;
  That eye and tongue and arm would strive in
    vain,
While all I sought to do was still undone.
  Not yet, not yet! Wilt not thou come again
When I have met my foes once more, and won
  The victory o'er pride, or greed, or lust,
  And know I have been something more than
    dust?

MARS HILL.

IF some time once before we close our eyes
  In death, to finite beings power could be
  One moment to put on infinity;
And at our will if we could break the guys
Which the events of by-gone centuries,
  Each in its narrow niche holds steadfastly;
  And, as we choose, in its completeness see
Some one grand view out of the past arise,
  How fain my feet would be to linger near
The streams and in the groves of Italy,
  That Virgil's living voice I might once hear;
Yet I would blind my eyes, if it must be,
  Lest they should look on that entrancing land,
  If so I might with Paul at Athens stand.

BLIND.

OH, happy bird, whose presence I feel near,
Whose thrilling notes fall sweetly on my ear,
    Though I mark not your sweep across the sky,
    Or splendor of your plumage, with my eye,
My heart leaps at your song, and knows its cheer.

Turn day to night through the slow-wasting year,
And spread your wings with ever-haunting fear,
    Among your trills would ever be a sigh,
        Oh, happy bird?

Could I reach out beyond the darkness here,
Which holds me helpless in this narrow sphere,
    And with your gift divine, of melody,
    Still with my song some sad heart's bitter cry,
Glad were the dusky hours, and life were dear,
        Oh, happy bird!

THEY WAIT THE MAIL.

THEY wait the mail,—one brown and spare,
One is a blonde, and plump and fair,—
   A dapper clerk runs to and fro,
   Each parcel boxes in its row,—
Knows he black eyes and blue are there?

While he is chirk and debonair,
Distributing with skill and care
   His messages of weal and woe,—
     They wait the mail.

Now one by one,—all on the square,—
Each in his turn is served his share;
   And still *they* linger,—do you know,—
   Is natty clerk the brunette's beau?
Or dallies he with golden hair?—
     They wait the *male*.

WHEN SHINES THE MOON.

WHEN shines the moon, at full, so bright,
Upon the earth with pale, sweet light,
  As bustling day lies in repose,
  And dewdrops dally with the rose,
How lovely is the summer night!

The stars that look from loftier height,—
How tremblingly they shrink from sight,
  Lost in the silver flood that flows,
    When shines the moon!

Oh, mellow moonlight, yellow-white,—
We love it, since we love the right;
  For wickedness and it are foes,
  Since crime is bold when moonlight goes,
And flees away an evil sprite,
    When shines the moon.

A BALLAD OF MY MARE.

COMING down to us from the ages back,
  Are richest treasures of legend and lore;
Of telling quaint truths they had a queer knack,
  And to-day there came to me o'er and o'er
An Arabic saying of long before,
  And it through my brain continually rang
As I galloped along the Owasco shore:
  "The joys of life in the forelock hang."

Metempsychosis, and all such clack,
  Our modern philosophers now ignore;
Yet I sometimes think we should place a smack
  Of truth to old heathen Pythagoras' score;
Then I dream of a comely maiden of yore,
  Who parted, maybe, with sorrowing pang
From the spirit that I in my mare adore,—
  "The joys of life in the forelock hang."

Great sorrow will fill that day, alack!
  When she and I are companions no more;
Her coat is like satin, glossy and black,
  It shines like the waistcoats our fathers wore;

On her polished neck hangs her mane galore,
    And I sing as never Sheik truer sang
Of steed that him long and faithfully bore,
    "The joys of life in the forelock hang."

ENVOY.

Don't look for a friend with naught to deplore,—
    The bite of a tooth now and then leaves a tang ;
Our quarrels break ties, our caresses restore,
    " Our joys of life in the forelock hang."

THE OLD MILL.

THE stream is small, the current is still,
    It winds between banks where the alders sway,
Then widens and deepens and flows to the mill
    Beyond,—one built in my grandsire's day ;
A quaint old dam holds the waters at bay,
    Then over they leap with deafening sound,
And angrily toss their foam and spray,
    As the great, strong wheel rolls round and round.

The stream is bridged at the foot of the hill,
 Where the trailing arbutus blooms in May,
And the tall, fierce briers with blackberries fill
 And ripen in summer's latest warm ray;
But from early morn to the twilight gray
 The whir of the stone, where the corn is ground,
And the hum of the saw are heard for aye,
 As the great, strong wheel rolls round and round.

Spruce, hemlock, and pine are carved up at will;
 Shaft, carriage, and saw the millers obey;
Rafter and plank and clapboard and sill
 From the round, big logs are sliced away,
And shaped at pleasure, as potters mould clay,
 And everywhere logs and lumber abound,
Piled up like cobs by the children in play,
 As the great, strong wheel rolls round and round.

ENVOY.

The years and the waters,—they never stay,
 Though the warp and filling of lives are wound,
And the millers succumb to Time's decay,
 As the great, strong wheel goes round and round.

THE BALLAD OF POVERTY.

No ranches or vineyards I call my own;
   Only castles of air are my palaces;
No lines of rail, or of telephone,
   No jewels in mines, or ships on the seas,
Are mine by right of the statute's decrees;
   But why need I grieve o'er my poverty?
I have wealth that never away from me flees,
   In those that I love, and in things that bless me.

Only yesterday the sunlight shone
   On the leafless boughs of the apple-trees;
To-day behold the bright blossoms blown!
   For a feast of their fragrance who asks for fees?
My right in their beauty who'll question or seize?
   Sky and mountain are mine, and river and sea,
And in thought I roam wherever I please,
   To those that I love, and things that bless me.

Free air I breathe as a king on his throne;
   I cringe to no man, nor bend my knees,
Save to the Master of all alone;
   He unlocks for me His treasuries,

16*

And I am heir to His legacies;
　A glimpse of the glories of heaven I see,—
Though the wine I drink has some earthly lees,—
　In those that I love, and in things that bless me.

ENVOY.

Friend, you and I follow our destinies;
　You have wealth, maybe; I am poor as needs be,
Excepting what riches are counted in these:
　In those that I love, and in things that bless me.

CHRISTINE.

I.

YOUR eyes are night, Christine,
　And ruddy morn, your lips;
Their flush is warm, I ween;
Your eyes are night, Christine,
I tremble at their sheen,
　Thrilled to my finger-tips;
Your eyes are night, Christine,
　And ruddy morn your lips.

II.

To make your cheek, Christine,
  White roses blend with red;
The wealth of both you glean
To make your cheek, Christine;
Eye has no fairer seen,
  And hearts are captive led;
To make your cheek, Christine,
  White roses blend with red.

III.

Ah, me! what grace, Christine,
  Like white clouds here and there,
Flecking a sky serene!
Ah, me! what grace, Christine,
Of neck and brow the screen
  Half hides of your brown hair!
Ah, me! what grace, Christine,
  Like white clouds here and there!

IV.

Pure as the snow, Christine,
  Fair as the summer, though,
With richest bloom and green;
Pure as the snow, Christine,

Your life makes mine more clean
 The more of it I know;
Pure as the snow, Christine,
 Fair as the summer, though.

VI.

Your speech is wine, Christine,
 And thrills me every draught
I drink with you, my queen!
Your speech is wine, Christine,
Yet makes my thirst grow keen
 With every beacon quaffed;
Your speech is wine, Christine,
 And thrills me every draught.

V.

Your years are few, Christine,
 While mine far on have rolled;
Wide yawns the gulf between;
Your years are few, Christine,
But on your love I lean;
 Bless you, sweet five-year-old!
Your years are few, Christine,
 While mine far on have rolled.

TO-DAY.

To-DAY the eyes are hot and blind with tears,
  To-day the heart is pierced and dead with
      sorrow ;
Love's whisper, mayhap, yesterday endears,
To-day the eyes are hot and blind with tears;
E'en though a shadow of the darkness clears
  Up in the white dream of divine to-morrow,
To-day the eyes are hot and blind with tears,
  To-day the heart is pierced and dead with
      sorrow.

THE END.